The Hands
They Were Dealt

The Hands
They Were Dealt

Inspirational Stories of
Overcoming the Odds

by
Mandy Penn

Volume 1

The Hands They Were Dealt, Volume 1: Inspirational Stories of
    Overcoming the Odds

ISBN 979-8-9897770-2-0 (Paperback)

Cover and Interior Design: Just Right Productions
Photography: Mandy Penn Photography

Volume 1, January 2024

Printed in physical and digital form
in the United States of America.

DEDICATION

To you, the reader… may you find hope in these stories and find the will and motivation to continue on and overcome whatever obstacles you may currently face or what may come in the future.

To my kids… I hope you learn how to work through your problems and overcome them, even when the outcome or future can look bleak and unfathomable.

TABLE OF CONTENTS

FOREWORD

As I sit down to write this, I can't help but feel a sense of excitement and awe. This book represents a perfect union of two of the most effective tools of communication: images and words. Images have always held a special place in my heart, whether it's the beauty of a landscape or the feelings captured in a portrait. They have a unique ability to convey complex ideas and emotions without the need for words. On the other hand, words have the power to inspire, motivate and transform us in ways we often cannot fathom. They can lift us up, give us hope and help us see the world in a whole new light.

This book is a beautiful exploration of the combined effectiveness of images and words. It's a collaboration that demonstrates how these two elements can work together to convey a passage that is both visually and emotionally compelling. It is a book that showcases the power of art and storytelling and how they can be used to create meaningful change in the world. Through the passionate stories of each author and the immersive visual art of Mandy Penn, what you are about to experience is going to take you to a whole other level.

As I read through the stories within this book, I found myself becoming caught up in the encounters of the authors, which drew me into a world of sentiment and experience. Each contributor has their own extraordinary story to tell and their own insights to share. These stories can be heart-wrenching while also uplifting and inspiring. Mandy's artwork is abstract, thought-provoking and evocative. Every piece in this book has been carefully crafted to create a powerfully emotional impact.

As a mindset coach, I have seen firsthand the potential these stories have in helping others shift their perspectives and overcome the challenges before them. When we are able to see a situation or circumstance from a different angle, it can open up new possibilities for growth and change. When we are able to connect with a story or an image on a deeper level, it can help us tap into our own inner wisdom and find the courage to persevere.

I am honored to be a part of this project, to have the opportunity to write this foreword, and to be able to share in the transcendence that happens when these images and stories are combined in such a beautiful way. This book represents the culmination of the hard work and dedication of many talented individuals. It is my belief that these images and writings will inspire and transform all who read them.

In a world where we are constantly bombarded with information and distractions, it's easy to become numb to the beauty and transformational capabilities of telling our stories. *The Hands They Were Dealt* is a reminder that when we take the time to tell our own hero's journey, we wield the power to rebuild the lives of others in ways we could never imagine. So, I invite you to sit back, relax and allow yourself to be engulfed in the magic of Mandy's imagery and the words of the contributors.

Dr. Garrett Goggans is an international best selling author, speaker and mindset coach who has heard people state that working toward success is like moving upstream without a paddle. It is his mission to help others see that with the proper mindset they can get up that proverbial stream with no paddle.

ACKNOWLEDGMENTS

First and foremost, thank you to my husband, kids and family for their continued support throughout this whole process. You all are such a great support system. I could not have done it without your faith and love.

Thank you to my amazing mindset coach, Garrett Goggans, for planting the seed about creating a book to showcase my artistic talent by portraying personal stories through imagery. Your guidance and unwavering belief in my abilities were instrumental, and I'm not sure I would have taken that significant step without your invaluable support.

A huge thank you to my photography and art mentor, Sandra Pearce, who helped me display the images in a way I didn't think possible. With your guidance I was able to depict the stories the way I envisioned. You are the most amazing and loving photography mentor I could ever ask for.

Thank you very much to my amazing editor, Jeff Scott Ruiz. You have been instrumental in navigating me through this process, and I am genuinely grateful for all the valuable input and guidance you have provided.

Thank you to my tribe (you know who you are). You have continued to support me in ways unimaginable.

Last but certainly not least, thank YOU, the reader. You have chosen to pick up this book and read a glimpse into some of our lives, I hope you find hope in the words you are about to read and the images you are about to see.

INTRODUCTION

Experiences play a pivotal role in shaping who we are, and they tell a unique story. It is essential to recognize that although two individuals may share a common issue such as depression, it can manifest differently for each of them. This understanding led me to create a book that allows people to share their stories—not only through words but also through powerful imagery. As a photographer, I've always believed that a picture is worth a thousand words. It can evoke a range of emotions, from heartache to joy and everything in between.

My goal is to provide a resource where people can read about others' experiences, how they've transformed their trauma into hope and turned the tide from darkness to light. Regardless of the cards we have been dealt, it's essential to acknowledge that everyone's experiences, big or small, are significant and should never be taken lightly. This book embodies that belief. It's a tribute to resilience and the strength to turn adversity into something positive. It reminds us that there's hope even in the darkest times.

Capturing these moments and narratives is at the core of what I do. This book has given me a remarkable opportunity to convey these stories in a way I never imagined. I'm immensely grateful to all the contributors and everyone involved. I look forward to continuing this journey and producing more volumes.

CHAPTER ONE

The Key to Hope: Chained to the NICU

Mandy Penn

When I was a child, I used to play "house." In my make-believe world, I was always the mom taking care of the babies. It was a game that hinted at my lifelong dream of nurturing. As I grew older, that dream led me to a career as a nanny. I loved that job, especially as I watched the children in my care grow and develop. As much as I cherished those moments, though, I had always known that one day I wanted to be a mother myself.

At 22, I married the most amazing man. Like many young couples, we thought we understood what love was; however, the first few years were challenging. We struggled to communicate effectively, and I had a habit of trying to push him away during conflicts. Fortunately, Caleb's unwavering determination to stay and work on our relationship became a cornerstone of our marriage. Our bond grew stronger as we learned to communicate and understand each other.

A few years down the road, we felt the time was right to start a family. At times, it was like a rollercoaster, and we were aware there might be obstacles to overcome; but one was specifically challenging. I had been diagnosed with polycystic ovarian syndrome (PCOS) at the age of 13, which added complexity to our family planning. PCOS made it difficult to predict my ovulation, and the uncertainty of timing weighed on us. I underwent numerous tests, and in November 2011, things took an unexpected turn. I took a pregnancy test, and it was positive! We were over-joyed and couldn't contain our excitement. We told everyone, embracing the idea of sharing our happiness with the world. However, at around ten weeks, we experienced a devastating setback: I had a miscarriage. The joy we had felt was swiftly replaced by sorrow.

This heart-wrenching experience brought us an unexpected gift—the comfort of knowing we weren't alone. Friends and family shared their own stories of miscarriages, offering empathy and understanding. Although the loss was difficult to bear, this shared sense of connection helped us cope.

In August 2012, Caleb and I talked to our doctor who informed us that we might want to reach out to a fertility doctor, since the tracking and the pills I was taking weren't helping. In September, I took my last dose of Clomid (an ovulation stimulator) and figured we would start our fertility journey in December. Surprisingly, in November, I discovered I was preg-nant again! Our excitement was again uncontainable, and we shared our joy with everyone, even against advice we were given to keep the news to ourselves this time around.

Nine weeks into the pregnancy, complications arose. Cramps and bleeding became a cause for concern. My anxiety reached new heights. We rushed to the doctor's office, hoping for the best, but they could not find a heartbeat. Our world started to crumble as we grappled with the idea of another loss.

The doctor scheduled an emergency ultrasound. While the tech con-ducted the procedure, my husband and I went back and forth from look-ing at each other to looking at the screen. This went on for a minute until Caleb pointed to the screen and asked, "So, is that like the front and the back of the baby?" To this, the tech responded, "Oh, no. You didn't know you were having twins?" I wasn't miscarrying, after all! The excessive hor-mones were due to the presence of two babies.

Around 29 weeks, I happened to be celebrating my sister's 18th birthday, her prom day, and getting her dance pictures taken. During breakfast, I began to experience contractions, which I initially attributed to the false labor symptoms of Braxton-Hicks. I started to count them, thinking it was a routine occurrence. However, the contractions intensified and became relentless. My aunt, a nurse, advised me to monitor them for an hour. The hours passed, and the contractions showed no signs of relenting. My aunt's concern grew, and she insisted we head to the hospital so they could try to prevent the babies from coming early.

As we headed to Penrose Saint Francis Hospital, I was very relaxed. I didn't think anything of it because it was too early for these babies to come out. I was thinking I'd just be on bed rest, but I was completely unaware of the life-altering events that were about to unfold. When we arrived, we were told that we were not in their computer system yet because pre-registration typically started at 33 weeks into pregnancy.

They connected me to a monitor, then filled out the necessary paperwork. Simultaneously, my mom contacted my husband, who was at work. She initially suggested he remain there since it didn't seem like a significant issue. However, he insisted on coming to the hospital. He believed it was essential to be there with his wife and their babies. At this stage, they hadn't examined me and were monitoring me via belly sensors.

My immediate response was to resist inducing the birth, believing it was too early and that my babies needed more time to develop. I was distressed by the situation and overwhelmed by pain and emotions. Doctor O'Connell arrived and comforted me, assuring me of my safety. They swiftly moved me to the operating room.

The surgery room was a scene of high-stakes drama. A local anesthesia provided a detachment from the unfolding events, but my heart and mind raced with questions. The surgeons had been working for a while, but there was an eerie silence in the room. *Shouldn't babies be crying when they come out?* I could not think of anything else other than why my babies were not crying. *What's going on? Are they alive?* I was so emotional about how fast this day was moving. At 9:00 am, we were eating breakfast. It was now 12:34 pm, and the babies were being delivered. Things continued to unfold so fast that I barely got to see them before the medical staff rushed them to the Neonatal Intensive Care Unit (NICU), sewed me back up and took me to recovery.

I vividly recall being wheeled into the NICU. My twin babies were in separate rooms, and I couldn't even touch them. They were connected to various machines, including an incubator, and they were intubated with cords running down their tiny throats. I noticed a pulse oximeter on their little feet. Honestly, they looked like little aliens to me.

I should have been filled with overwhelming joy, but I felt an unexpected wave of nausea, and tears welled up in my eyes. This wasn't the beautiful, heartwarming moment I had imagined of my babies being born perfectly healthy. They were relying on the dedicated nurses (who were true lifesavers) to care for them. At that moment, both Caleb and I felt utterly helpless.

It took me five days in the hospital to recover from the C-section. During that time, the NICU staff became our lifeline. They not only offered remarkable medical care, but also unwavering emotional support. Throughout our challenging NICU journey, they were a source of hope. We experienced a rollercoaster of emotions as we celebrated small milestones, from the first time we held our babies to their incremental developmental progress. However, the policy which limited our interactions with the babies due to their sensitivity was heart-wrenching. As a new mother, it left me yearning for more physical contact.

After my discharge, we returned home to an empty nursery. We had nothing to show for the ordeal we'd been through, and I was heartbroken. I spent hours in bed, crying my eyes out. Caleb was incredibly supportive, and he allowed me to pour out my emotions. He has always been there for me when I needed him. However, work and other responsibilities were now pulling at him, and he needed to get back to those duties. I respected his decision, even though I felt like I needed to be at the hospital 24/7.

The first time we got to hold our babies was on day three, after they came out of the incubator. I couldn't do much in those early days—no diaper changes, no feeding, and just a gentle touch now and then. I couldn't help but wonder how this had become my life. The NICU experience, whether short or long (as ours was) was a wild and emotional ride.

My emotions were all over the place. One day I'd feel hopeful, and the next I'd be down. The continuous alarms and atmosphere in the NICU made it even harder. People often take smooth deliveries for granted and don't realize what else could happen until they're in the thick of it. I had an incredible support system—the nurses, my husband, my mom, and my best friend, Paige.

I tried to navigate a surreal world where those tiny miracles are connected to wires and monitors, their fragile bodies requiring constant medical attention. The beeping of machines is a disconcerting soundtrack and a reminder of the fragility of life. It's a surreal dance between hope and despair as small victories are celebrated only to have the next challenges overshadow them. Each day is a delicate balance between hope and fear, progress and setbacks.

The NICU became a second home; the constant hum of machines and the sterile scent became oddly familiar. The emotional toll on parents is immense. They deal with moments of joy at the slightest sign of improvement and heart-wrenching anxiety when faced with setbacks. The helplessness of watching their babies fight for survival is a weight that lingers, casting a long shadow even after leaving.

Trauma extends beyond the NICU. Parents grapple with guilt, questioning if there was anything they could have done differently. The separation from their infants during those crucial early days leaves an indelible mark on the parent-child bond. The trauma manifests in various ways, from anxiety about the children's health to an overprotective instinct that stems from the fear of losing them.

As our twins grow, so does the realization of the developmental hurdles they may face. Milestones become not just celebrations but also markers of potential delays. The fear of the unknown also persists, creating an emotional undercurrent in the daily lives of both the children and their parents.

During this challenging period, I turned to journaling as an emotional outlet. I had never been a consistent diarist; I was typically the person who would get a new diary, write in it for two days then never use it again. However, the NICU journey inspired me to start. I recorded my thoughts, emotions and experiences daily. This journal served as a way to process my trauma and maintain a connection with my babies when I couldn't be by their side. Little did I know this journal would become a source of inspiration for not only myself, but for others as well.

I had the journal printed into an album consisting of photos and detailed medical terms, along with my daily entries. I gave one of three copies to the NICU in the hope that it could help others understand their journeys. I believe they've shown it to patients a few times.

Recently, a friend of mine was going through a tough time. Her twins were in the NICU, so I gave her a copy. I wasn't sure how much it would help, but she told me it brought her clarity and was incredibly thankful. It's fascinating how a story I never thought needed telling has helped me connect with others.

Caleb was the only person who could talk sense into me. He had reassured me the babies were in good hands, and I was eventually able to leave and not feel chained to those incubators. The NICU experience became a chapter in my family's story. It left scars, but it also imparted a profound appreciation for life's fragility. That trauma is now met with resilience, fostering a sense of gratitude for each milestone achieved. It's a testament to the human spirit's ability to endure, adapt and find light even in the darkest moments.

I am now a photographer. One of the greatest things about my business is taking pictures of newborns. I truly believe my journey has given me special insight into this part of my job. As a newborn photographer, I can relate to clients and apply the lessons I learned in the NICU. I love what I do, and I would never change it for the world.

In the end, the NICU experience made us stronger, more compassionate and deeply appreciative of the precious moments in life. Our twins are now ten years old; they are a testament to resilience and the enduring power of love. My journey as a mother, photographer and storyteller has given me a unique perspective on life's challenges and the importance of sharing our stories.

I have chosen to share my story so it can offer insight into the emotional journey of NICU parents. Every story matters regardless of the challenges we face. Our experiences shape who we are. Mine have enabled me to understand the importance of empathy, compassion and the strength of the human spirit. They have made me a better photographer and a better person.

Mandy Penn draws her inspiration from the vibrant tapestry of life woven through the telling of others' stories. An impassioned photographer and artist, she channels her love for humanity into capturing moments that resonate with the raw authenticity of the human experience.

As a devoted member of the Professional Photographers of America, Professional Photographers of Colorado, and the Professional Photographers of Colorado Springs guild, Mandy has established herself as a luminary in the field. Her dedication and talent have earned her the prestigious "Best of the Springs" accolade for an impressive five consecutive years. Recognized as a Master Craftsman through the Professional Photographers of America, Mandy continually refines her craft, pushing the boundaries of her artistry.

Mandy's work has garnered attention on national platforms, including features on *Good Morning America, POPSUGAR, Sad Panda* and more. Her ability to capture the essence of human emotion has made her a sought-after artist, and her lens serves as a conduit for the profound stories that unfold before it.

In her words and images, Mandy Penn invites you to join her on a captivating exploration of the human spirit.

Mandy is married to an amazing and supportive husband. They have two amazing 10-year-olds who are an inspiration to their lives.

For an intimate look into Mandy's world and to stay connected with her artistic journey, be sure to follow her at www.mandypenn.com.

CHAPTER TWO

My Son, My Angel

Jessie Branford

"I am so sorry. There was nothing we could do."

Those are words no parent should ever hear about their child, but it was my reality.

On March 6, 2016, my life changed forever. My beautiful son, Aiden Clark Branford, was born at 9:20 pm. My pregnancy was easy. I hadn't suffered morning sickness and only gained minimal weight. Overall, I felt great; I loved being pregnant. I felt more beautiful in my pregnant body than I had ever felt before. I went into natural labor at 38 weeks and 5 days with only 12 hours of labor.

I was officially a mom! It was something I had always wanted and dreamed about. Aiden was the most incredible baby and little boy. He was calm and happy and slept through the night as early as 4 weeks. His dimples lit up a room and melted my heart, as well as anyone else's he met.

Aiden was an adventurer. He never left the house without his best friend, a bunny named Puppy. He loved trips to the zoo with mommy, going to gymnastics with Bubby and rock climbing with Daddy. He loved helping Daddy plant and harvest in our home garden; it was a great excuse to dig in the dirt and play in the water. He loved watching movies and dancing to the songs on the screen. He loved collecting character figures and lining them all up, carefully facing them all in the same direction. He loved snow days which often included sledding, building snowmen and making snow ice cream. He loved making crafts at Home Depot on the first Saturday of every month. He loved going camping in the summers and seeing the hot air balloons every Labor Day weekend. He loved the holidays. We'd dress up as a family for Halloween and go trick-or-treating. We made cookies for Santa and decorated the tree and lit candles for Hanukkah. We enjoyed fireworks on the 4th of July. Most of all, he loved Easter because of the egg treasure hunt.

As he got older, one of his favorite things became geocaching and hunting for treasures. I used to tell people that "one man's trash is Aiden's treasure." We would find Aiden's treasures everywhere—in his pockets, in the car, in the yard and all over our house! Every so often, I would sit down with him to sort through all the treasures and decide what was truly a treasure worth keeping and what was trash we could throw away. Some of the best treasures he found were deer antlers in the open spaces around our neighborhood.

As Aiden grew up, he developed a "never met a stranger" personality. He was so outgoing and made new friends everywhere he went. He loved letting himself into our neighbors' homes and visiting with them. It certainly helped that many of them offered him candy or a treasure as part of his visit.

Aiden had a giving heart. During the COVID-19 pandemic, Aiden was desperate to host a lemonade stand. We set up a canopy in our driveway and invited friends and family to join us, all masked and socially distanced. Aiden was so excited to make and sell his "lemonlade," as he called it. We wanted him to understand the importance of giving to others, especially during COVID, and encouraged him to keep some money and donate the majority. We chose to donate the money to our local food bank, Care and Share Food Bank of Southern Colorado. Aiden was able to raise $110, which translated to 880 meals for families in our community. We hand delivered the cash to a friend of ours who works at the food bank and got a tour of the beautiful facility. It made a lasting impact on Aiden, our family and our community.

Aiden lived every moment of his life to the very fullest. Sometimes I wonder if he knew his time on Earth was limited and if he knew he had to make an impact quickly.

The Day That Changed My Life

On June 3, 2021, my entire world came crashing down around me.

Earlier that day, Aiden had some extensive dental work done and I wasn't sure if he was going to feel up for going to gymnastics that afternoon. Ultimately, he decided he wanted to go, and I was so excited to finally be able to see what he was learning. My mom always took Aiden to gymnastics, but that day my husband and I were able to be there with him. We got there a little early that afternoon and waited for my husband to meet us. My husband arrived just in time for Aiden's class to begin. Aiden, as always, was so excited to see his daddy.

Aiden's younger brother, Oliver, was already loaded in his stroller, and Aiden was standing next to my car when my husband pulled into the parking lot. Aiden said hi to Daddy in his truck while I went to get Oliver. As I waited for my husband to park, a stranger in the parking lot casually asked me, "Is this your son?" At that point, I realized Aiden was no longer next to me, and I went to see what this man was asking about.

As soon as I saw Aiden I let out the most bloodcurdling scream I have ever made or heard. Aiden was lying face down in the middle of the parking lot in a pool of his own blood. I raced over to him among bystanders who were starting to gather. I don't remember the exact order of what happened next, but I do remember the following: My husband called 911. Multiple strangers began performing CPR on my son while I stabilized his head. Someone brought an AED from the library and began hooking Aiden up to it. Another stranger moved Oliver, in his stroller, away from

The Hands They Were Dealt

the scene while trying to keep him calm. Eventually, the firetruck, police officers and ambulance arrived.

Aiden had been hit by a vehicle in the parking lot. What complicated our situation was that the person driving the vehicle was my husband.

Aiden was rushed to the hospital by ambulance. ALONE. Because of his critical condition, I was not allowed to ride in the ambulance with him. Eventually, after answering some investigative questions by the police (and using a water bottle to wash the blood off my hands), I was escorted by police car to the hospital. My husband was required to stay on scene to answer more questions.

The ride to the hospital was excruciating. I don't know why, but the police officer drove to the hospital without sirens. Why did he drive so slowly?! Why was he unable to tell me anything about Aiden's status? I remember thinking on the way to the hospital that no news was good news, but I also knew after holding Aiden in that parking lot that his chances of survival were incredibly dim. If he did survive, his quality of life would never be the same.

I finally arrived at the hospital and was quickly introduced to the hospital chaplain. The police officer with whom I rode did not leave my side. I am not an incredibly religious person. I was raised Jewish, but I connect more to the religion culturally than religiously. The idea of sitting with a chaplain was uncomfortable for me; but as the night progressed, I became incredibly grateful for her guidance and support.

I was in a complete state of shock, which was quickly becoming anger. No one was telling me anything about Aiden's status.

At some point, after what felt like an eternity since arriving at the hospital, the chaplain took me to see Aiden. "Mom is here!" exclaimed the doctors and nurses. To me, that was a clear signal among themselves that I was not supposed to see or hear what was happening in that room. My 5-year-old son was splayed, naked and lifeless, on his back on a table surrounded by at least 20 doctors and nurses. The looks on their faces revealed immense sadness and defeat. I was quickly ushered out of that operating room and moved to a private waiting room. I was still with the escorting police officer and the hospital chaplain. My husband and the rest of my family had yet to make it to the hospital, although I think I had called them already to tell them to come.

Within a few minutes after seeing Aiden lifeless on the operating table, a doctor came into the private waiting room to deliver the news to me that Aiden had not survived his injuries. The rest of my conversation with that doctor was a blur. I was still alone and without anyone I knew who could provide any kind of comfort.

In retrospect, I remained incredibly calm while receiving the worst news of my life. I was absolutely in a state of shock, and all I could think about was who to call and what steps needed to be taken next.

We sat in that private waiting room at the hospital for about four hours after Aiden died. During that time, we were joined by my husband, Oliver, my parents and my in-laws, as well as my two best friends. We sat in silence and cried. I repeatedly assured my husband this was not his fault. We asked so many what-if questions, reminisced and eventually had the opportunity to say good-bye to Aiden.

Our waiting room was connected to a second waiting room. They wheeled Aiden into the connecting room and gave those of us who wanted it the opportunity to see him again and say our good-byes. Aiden's death was an active investigation. Because of this, we were not allowed to be alone with him as we said our final good-byes. We were supervised by a police officer while we sobbed over his dead body.

We held Aiden's hand, the only thing we were allowed to touch, and told him how much we loved him and missed him. We told him how sorry we were that his life ended so early and abruptly. We told him how grateful we were to have had the time we did with him. We told him we would

The Hands They Were Dealt

always keep his memory alive. We said the Mourner's Kaddish, a traditional Jewish prayer, over his body. It was awful but necessary. I initially wondered if I wanted to see him in that state, but I am so glad I was able to get a bit of closure in that moment.

When we were ready, we gathered our belongings and went home to begin our lives without our son. How are you ever ready to leave the hospital without your loved ones, knowing you will never see them again? We were sent home empty handed. Because Aiden's death was an active investigation, his personal belongings were held in police custody. This wasn't like the movies where you see people leaving with a transparent bag of clothes, shoes and jewelry. We had nothing of Aiden's. We were, however, given business cards and pamphlets for people and places we could, should or needed to call: the morgue, funeral homes, police officers and investigators, chaplains, mental health services, etc.

I experienced a bittersweet sigh of relief when we got back to my car that evening and saw that Aiden's best friend, Puppy, was in the car and not in police custody. My husband and I were comforted to know we still had a small part of Aiden we could hold and smell forever, just like Aiden always did when he was sad.

Throughout the evening and following weeks, my husband and I were asked questions about the moments that led up to the accident. The night of the accident, my husband was required to provide a blood sample to prove that drugs and alcohol were not a factor. We had several phone calls with the police officer in charge of our case.

Later in the summer, we were able to meet with the lead police officer and share stories about Aiden. The officer shared with us how deeply our case impacted him. Once the case was closed, he personally delivered to us Aiden's neon green Crocs he had been wearing the day of the accident. These were special to us because he and Oliver had a matching pair. Overall, they determined this was truly a terrible freak accident.

During those first days and weeks, I often asked myself the dreaded "what if" questions. Did the dental work that morning cause Aiden to be more unsteady on his feet? Why didn't we skip gymnastics that day like I had initially planned? How would I have felt if someone else was driving the vehicle that hit him? Through my time in counseling, I have been able to stop asking myself these questions and stop trying to make sense of this tragedy. It was just that—a terrible tragedy. There is no why. Aiden's death is out of order. It will never make sense.

In the days following the accident, we endured what no parents should ever have to—planning their child's funeral. The morning after, I had woken to my new reality and had a full-blown panic attack (my first and only). Within 24 hours after the accident, my husband and I took Xanax to take some of the edge off. It upset me that we had to take time to meet with our doctor about this prescription rather than being sent home with it from the hospital.

We began the daunting task of calling close friends to inform them about Aiden's death. We wrote and delivered an announcement letter to mailboxes in our elderly neighborhood, many of whom do not have social media. We were inundated with lasagnas and BBQ. We selected a funeral home. We signed the paperwork to have his body transferred from the morgue. We decided to have his body cremated rather than buried.

We sat with Aiden one last time before the cremation. This was another incredibly difficult decision. The funeral home had prepared his body for a viewing, but I was so worried to see him again in that state. At the time, I didn't want to remember him that way. My mom was sure she wanted to see him again, so I asked her to go in first and let me know if she thought I could handle seeing him that way. Ultimately, I made the decision to see him again because I didn't want to regret not seeing him and wondering what that moment would have been like. When I walked into the room, I was completely shocked by how beautiful he was. The funeral home did such an incredible job covering up his injuries. Aiden was known for his long, beautiful hair, and we got to see it and touch it one last time. We got to hold his hand and touch his face. It was exactly what I needed.

Aiden's cremains reside in a treasure box on our fireplace mantle with Puppy watching over. Making the decision to cremate or bury a child is not something most parents plan for. No parent should ever experience the death of a child, especially one taken so young and tragically. Aiden belongs with us, not buried underground. I know this decision was the best for us.

My two best friends who were with us at the hospital were so helpful in those first few days and weeks. They helped make phone calls, deliver letters, take care of Oliver, set up a meal train and a GoFundMe page, and they gave us a shoulder to cry on or just sat in silence with us. I will never be able to adequately thank them for the support they gave us then and continue to give us now. That can also be said about our entire community of friends and family. The way people supported us with love, food, cards and monetary donations was monumental.

Aiden's celebration of life took place 10 days after his death. It was a beautiful day for such a tragic event, and it was standing room only. Hundreds of people attended the service in person and on Zoom in bright colors to celebrate Aiden's short but powerful life. There were photos, music, tears and laughter. After the service, we gathered at a nearby park where people painted rocks to keep or share, something Aiden loved to do and find. We ate white donuts, one of Aiden's favorite treats, and were surrounded by so much love.

For five days after Aiden's funeral, we observed the Jewish tradition of sitting *shiva*, the Jewish period of mourning which typically lasts seven days. As Reform Jews, we structured this to match our wants, needs and beliefs. There were many traditions we did not observe during this time, but we wanted to devote time to grieving Aiden's death and beginning our healing journey. Living in a very Christian city, it was special to share this tradition with so many friends. During those five days, we were hardly ever alone. We ended up with more food than we could ever eat, especially during a time when we didn't really want to eat. We laughed and cried and reminisced about how much Aiden was loved and the impact he made on so many people in his incredibly short life. It was a beautiful transition into the difficult journey of living our lives without our son.

A Year of Firsts

If you have ever experienced the loss of a loved one, you know the first year is the most difficult—first heavenly birthday, holidays, "deathiversary," etc. Our first year without Aiden was spent in survival mode. I learned to take everything one breath, one minute, one day at a time. I learned that I *can* do hard things, even though I don't want to. I got my first tattoo, a picture of Aiden's best friend, Puppy, with Aiden's handwritten name. I survived my first trip to the zoo without Aiden, hearing triggering songs and seeing his empty car seat in the rear view mirror before eventually taking it out altogether.

My younger son, Oliver, saved my life in those first few days and months after Aiden died. I never truly had suicidal thoughts, though I often dreamed of being with Aiden again; however, those thoughts were short lived because I still had another beautiful son to live for. Oliver gave me a reason to continue breathing and get out of bed every morning. He forced me to eat when I had to make food for him. He helped me laugh and smile when it felt impossible. He held me in his tiny arms when I was sad. He truly brightened my life during such darkness.

One of the most difficult days I experienced after losing Aiden was my first day back to work. I am a teacher. Aiden died at the beginning of my summer break, and I thankfully already had some "time off" work. Before he died, I interviewed for a teaching position at a new school, our home school, where Aiden was supposed to attend kindergarten. As a teacher,

I always wanted my kids to go to the school where I taught. My husband always wanted our kids to go to the school he went to as a child. This new job was the best of both worlds. I was unofficially offered the new job on a Wednesday. Aiden died the next day, Thursday, and I got the official offer from HR on Friday.

I went from the highest of highs to the lowest of lows within 24 hours. How was I supposed to make this decision? Did I want to start over where I didn't know anyone? Could I return to the school where students would be asking about Aiden? Could I be without Aiden in the school he was supposed to attend? Ultimately, I decided to take the job at the new school because I still had the opportunity to be there with Oliver when he was old enough.

My first day back to work after summer was excruciating. I was leaving Oliver for the first time since Aiden died. I was walking into a building I didn't know with people I didn't know. Most of the staff knew that Aiden died over the summer, so I didn't have to explain this to them, but I didn't want that to define me as a person. I was terrified people would ask the dreaded question, "How are you doing?" and I wouldn't know how to respond. I had to remove myself a few times from the back-to-school activities to cry in my box-filled classroom.

I told my students about Aiden on the second day of school. For them to understand who I was as a person and a teacher, they needed to know Aiden was a part of my life. They expressed so much compassion and sympathy. A lot of them connected my loss to that of a lost pet. I needed them to know about Aiden so they could better understand if I needed to take time off or if I came to class feeling sad. I ended up taking at least one day off on the 3rd of every month, the monthly anniversary of Aiden's death. Those days were just too painful, and my emotions were unpredictable. I often spent those days holding Oliver close or practicing self-care, both of which were critical in making it through that school year.

To my surprise, and that of many others, I completed that school year. To this day, I still do not know how I managed. The thought never crossed my mind to not return to school, and I do not regret teaching that year. I needed the distraction and routine of teaching. I needed to be surrounded by people. It was incredibly difficult emotionally and mentally, but I truly needed to be at work. I was so proud of myself for making it through that school year and for making the difficult decision to take a leave of absence the following year. It was important to take time to focus on my mental health and give myself time to grieve and heal.

During that first year, I knew many days would be harder than others—monthly anniversaries, Thanksgiving, Christmas, his first Heavenly birthday, etc. It was important for me to make time during the day—whether five minutes or multiple hours—to remember Aiden. This included wearing his favorite color (orange) or having Puppy close by, or doing something I knew he would have enjoyed. The day I was most worried about was his birthday. My counselor suggested organizing a way to give back to our community on his birthday, and it was one of the best pieces of advice I received. It has now become a tradition to gather in our orange shirts with our friends and family to volunteer in our community. It is healing to help and support other people in Aiden's memory.

The days and moments I planned for and expected to be difficult were not often as hard as I thought. I imagined not being able to get out of bed on those days or crying all day, but I was pleasantly surprised I was able to function much better than anticipated. One day I had not anticipated as being difficult was New Year's Eve. It was one of the most difficult firsts I experienced. Obviously, this is not a very kid-centered holiday. I thought we would get dressed up, go to the symphony, count down to the new year and go to sleep. I did not realize this holiday symbolized a new beginning, moving into a new calendar year that Aiden would never experience. It felt so wrong to exist in a year he would not live in. The pain that evening was completely unexpected and overwhelming, but like all the other heartbreaking firsts, I survived.

During the *shiva* for Aiden, a very good friend of mine approached me to ask how I would feel about planning a 5k Fun Run in honor and memory of Aiden which would take place around the first anniversary of his death. She wanted the event to be a way of providing us comfort during what we all expected to be an excruciating time, and it would also give back to our community through Aiden's memory. I was honored and humbled that someone loved us and Aiden so much to even think about something like this. It was an easy choice, and Aiden's Adventure 5k was created as a local non-profit.

The first annual Aiden's Adventure 5k took place on June 4, 2022, one day after the first anniversary of his death. We were joined by over 250 people, both in-person and virtually from across the continent. We were surrounded by love and a sea of orange. Participants painted rocks, collected treasure boxes and released butterflies. Through registration fees, sponsors and donations, we raised a total of $8,500 which we donated to two local non-profits that were special to Aiden. This event truly became a day to look forward to instead of dread. It was the perfect way to celebrate and remember him.

Tragedy to Triumph

My husband and I are both "only children." When I was pregnant with Aiden, we decided that we only wanted to have one child. We enjoyed being only children and were provided with many opportunities we would not likely have had with siblings. We wanted to provide the same experience for Aiden; however, when he was about two and a half, I started thinking about my aging parents. As an only child, it is my sole responsibility to care for them as they grow older. This is a difficult task that I didn't want Aiden to bear on his own.

My husband and I decided we wanted to try for another baby. We got pregnant rather quickly, but we suffered a miscarriage at 13 weeks. I experienced what they call a missed miscarriage. My body did not present any signs or symptoms that our fetus had died, yet I was told at a scheduled doctor's appointment that there was no heartbeat. Prior to this experience, I didn't know this existed, and it came as quite a shock. Because I was already 13 weeks pregnant, my husband and I elected to deliver the fetus at the hospital rather than at home. This ended up being the best decision because I did not naturally deliver the placenta and required a D&C.

Our miscarriage was one of the most difficult and painful experiences we had encountered prior to Aiden's death. We learned and grew so much through the experience. We were comforted by many friends and family members who lifted us up and helped us move forward. When we were cleared to try again, we were fortunate to get pregnant rather quickly. Our second son, Oliver James Branford, was born on March 4, 2020, at 4:52 pm, just two days shy of Aiden's 4th birthday. Fun fact: I actually had the same due date forecasted for both of them!

Aiden died when Oliver was 15 months old. I remember immediately wondering if my husband and I would or should have another baby. It was a conversation we had together within the first 24 hours of Aiden's death. We had clearly decided before Oliver was born that we did not want Aiden to be an only child, and now we were faced with Oliver being raised as an only child. No child would ever replace Aiden, and having another baby was a decision we really needed to think about and process.

Throughout my first year of counseling, having another baby was a common discussion. I decided I needed to experience the first year without Aiden as clearly as possible. I did not want my grief to be clouded by hormones and the joy of pregnancy, but I also knew my biological clock was ticking. My husband and I began trying for another baby as soon as we passed the first anniversary of Aiden's death. Fortunately, we had

The Hands They Were Dealt

always gotten pregnant quickly, and this time was no exception. We found out we were pregnant just two months after the first anniversary of Aiden's death.

This pregnancy was incredibly difficult mentally. After having suffered a previous miscarriage, I knew that another one was certainly a possibility. Could I survive the loss of another baby while still grieving Aiden's death? This question was something I had to process and come to terms with before deciding to get pregnant again. Ultimately, I concluded that if I could survive Aiden's death, I could survive anything.

The pregnancy was full of anxiety until I could feel the baby moving. My blood pressure in the doctor's office was always high while anticipating that precious heartbeat. I monitored my blood pressure at home for the entirety of my pregnancy. Overall, they were fine until the end of my pregnancy when I developed gestational hypertension. I was induced at 37 weeks and 3 days, but once our new baby was in my arms, my anxiety subsided.

We did not know the gender of our babies during each pregnancy, and this was no exception. Before we got pregnant, I thought I needed to know so I could process and prepare myself for the possibility of having another son. After I got pregnant, this didn't seem as important, especially since Oliver already showed many similarities to Aiden. A healthy baby was all I wanted, and gender truly did not matter.

We were beyond thrilled to welcome our beautiful daughter, Amelia Louise Branford, on April 10, 2023. She weighed 7 pounds 3 ounces and was 19 inches long. My religious beliefs have not changed much over the last two years, but I do feel more connected to the spiritual world. I need to believe I will see Aiden again someday. I want to believe he hand-picked Amelia to join our family. I want to believe he met her before we did. I need to believe Aiden knew exactly what we needed to help mend our broken hearts.

Amelia will never replace Aiden, but she has certainly brought so much joy back into our lives. Oliver is a wonderful big brother. He loves to help feed her, hold her and help her with her pacifier. He often asks, "Where is MY baby?" if she is not nearby and gets very excited to see her after he has spent the day with his grandparents.

One of the things I grieved most about Aiden's death was a sibling relationship that Oliver would not experience, something my husband and I also did not have. I am incredibly grateful that Oliver and Amelia will now be able to grow up together. There will never be a day we don't think about or talk about Aiden. Oliver and Amelia will grow up knowing the amazing big brother they had and the guardian angel who now watches over them.

I knew after Aiden died that I wanted to share my vulnerability and be as transparent as I could about this journey. Losing a child is unfathomable. It is such a profound loss that at times it feels impossible to grieve and survive. If I have learned anything through this experience, it is to take everything one moment at a time. Be present. Love hard. Have grace. To experience this kind of grief means I also experienced great love. Every day I choose to be strong and resilient. It is not a decision I ever wanted to make, but for me it is the only way.

I will continue to grieve and heal for the rest of my life. Some days will continue to be harder than others, but I believe those days will come less often. I am forever grateful for the time I had with Aiden, though it was much too short. I know I am a better person because I got to be his mom.

I end with a quote from the musical, *Wicked:*

> *"Some people come into our lives for a reason, bringing something*
> *we must learn... Because I knew you [Aiden],*
> *I have been changed for good."*

Jessie Branford, a devoted resident of Colorado Springs, Colorado, resides with her husband and cherished children. Armed with a bachelor's degree in Human Development and Family Studies from Colorado State University, Jessie's passion for fostering growth and connection shines through her dynamic background. Having dedicated 14 years to shaping young minds as an elementary school teacher, she now gracefully embraces her role as a stay-at-home mom.

Jessie finds solace in her love for reading and an enduring wanderlust for travel. She marks her literary debut with this publication, a promising beginning in what is sure to be a prolific writing journey.

Jessie can be reached via facebook.com/jessie.branford and instagram.com/jessiebranford. Also visit Aiden's Adventure 5k on Facebook or www.aidensadventure5k.com for more information about this incredible non-profit dedicated to giving back to Aiden's community.

CHAPTER THREE

Four Hundred and Sixty-Five

Shannon Coker

It was roughly thirty years ago on a mild summer evening in Colorado at my childhood home. The lawn was immaculately landscaped, and I remember having spent hours upon hours weeding, gardening and manicuring. I vividly remember enjoying the crisp Colorado air as I sat on the front stoop with my mother, brother and stepfather.

My brother was probably playing a game of some sort. I don't recall which, but that's often what he did. My mother was sitting in a nearby patio chair. I remember both my arms and hands behind me, which were bracing me up since I had nothing to lean against. My large, oversized body was there for the world to see—notably, my mother.

"Shannon, suck it in." Her words were seared into my memory, as if sucking it in would help conceal my fat rolls and obesity, two things no child should have at that age. I had gotten used to it. I remember thinking as a child that I was just big-boned. I justified being overweight as a marker for uniqueness. I don't remember feeling like anything else set me apart from the crowd, but my size sure did.

It didn't really click until I was older that my size was a result of an addiction to food. It was my coping mechanism since childhood which resulted in obesity. Food never disappointed me, never bullied me or neglected me; it only offered comfort. After years of therapy and reflection, I discovered that my first memory of food and how it soothed me was as a teenager.

My older brother and I are just 18 months apart, and we fought very often as children. Rough housing was all part of being the younger sister. I remember having an emotional moment one day and found myself in the kitchen to help me feel better. Mom was baking peanut butter cookies and had thrown the scraps into the trash. As I went to throw something else away, I opened the top of the trash can and saw small balls of dough. Despite mainstream media telling us not to eat raw cookie dough, it's actually some of the best comfort food. I wondered why someone would trash perfectly good food scraps. I threw my own trash away and went to my room.

As I sat there, I fixated on that cookie dough. I couldn't get my brain to stop thinking it would give me comfort. After a few minutes had passed, I softly and gently tip-toed upstairs to the kitchen, gently removed the dough from the trash can and scurried back down to my room. I savored that dough. It delivered what I knew it would, and it gave me comfort. To this day, I still struggle when I think about eating peanut butter cookies.

I just got bigger as the years passed. Buying clothes was always a challenge. As a teenager, I don't remember shopping in the girls' section. It was always the women's and plus-size sections, so I felt relegated to dressing like a grandma. I was a school athlete and thought that my size shouldn't define me, so I continued with athletics as best I could. I loved playing volleyball and basketball and was one heck of a shotput and discus thrower (if I do say so myself); but even those memories are not immune to the shame my size inflicted on me.

I think back to volleyball tryouts and the dreaded one-mile run which was part of the evaluation. I couldn't fake my way around Prospect Lake, where the run took place. One loop was one mile. One start, one end, no shortcuts. Every day, ahead of track practice and the team gathering, each team member was supposed to run two warmup laps to stretch before we'd break off into our specialties. I would either intentionally be late to practice and run only one lap, or I'd be super early and get "caught" finishing my second lap, which was fake. My stamina could not handle circling the track twice.

I was a really good discus thrower, though. I was best in the region year after year and was a state qualifier in my junior and senior years. I was even recruited to throw in college. My goal, however, was not to improve on the actual sport. All I could think about was how to cheat my way out of circling that track. I lied so many times and always assumed my teammates could see right through me. If I were to ask any of my track or volleyball teammates about it, I'm sure they wouldn't remember that about me; they'd probably remember all the good stuff I did. To this day, I still carry the shame of openly cheating.

Decades later, I realized that all those childhood experiences—removing cookie dough from the trash can, being told to "suck it in," being as active as I could in school sports or student council   —were coverups to bigger issues within myself. Zero self-love, a complex relationship with my body, feeling unworthy, defining myself as a cheater and being addicted to food were all insulating me. Metaphorically, the hundreds of excess pounds of fat on my body did the exact same thing. It was my shield.

As a young adult, I no longer fit into chairs, car seats or airplane seats. So, the yo-yo dieting started. I tried Atkins, keto, low carb, high protein… Name a diet, and I did it. Once I realized I was addicted to food, I realized I needed to begin advocating for myself, or else I'd have a very short life.

Shortly after college, I went to my first Ob-Gyn appointment. I was diagnosed with polycystic ovarian syndrome (PCOS), a hormonal disorder caused by enlarged ovaries with small cysts on the outer edges. The doctor did not have any answers for me, but I remember two statements that day: "Conceiving a child will be extremely difficult, although not impossible," and "Your weight will always be challenging to manage due to your hormonal fluctuations." Naturally, I went online to learn more about it. I remember reading the words that described me perfectly: *PCOS can cause missed or irregular menstrual periods, excess hair growth, acne, infertility and weight gain.* It all pointed to having high levels of testosterone in the body and causing significant hormonal imbalances. There is relief in learning of a diagnosis, but there is also dread that surrounds overwhelming odds. I was the only one who could help me, and I knew I needed to go to war with my own body.

I found a doctor in Colorado Springs who specialized in women's care and PCOS. He was the first step in my journey to reclaim my body. Dr. Foley took one look at me in his office that day and said, "I don't need to do tests to know you have PCOS. I can look at you, and your physical appearance tells me you do."

I was both relieved and broken. Relieved because I found someone who could help, and broken because of how overweight I was. He asked how long I had been overweight, and speculated that it probably started back in high school and exacerbated itself when my hormones started raging. He was right, of course. He stated how my young adulthood could have been very different had my size been addressed back then. He told me I could have had a fighting chance when I was younger and smaller to help contain the hormonal imbalance and weight.

I'm an open book, and I was pretty vocal about my journey. One of my friends was a local news reporter who had just moved to town. She asked if she could share my story, as I had been losing a lot of weight under Dr. Foley's direction. I referred to that period of my journey as *#projectlose-weight* on social media. Sadly, it was temporary, and I remember hitting a plateau.

If you've ever dieted or tried to change your lifestyle when it comes to food, you know when you stop seeing results that it can play mental games. I had lost about a hundred pounds and gained it all back in a few short months. Once again, my narrative was filled with shame and disappointment, but this time it was publicized. It was all recollected when news snippets surfaced in my Facebook Memories feed. The scale continued to climb. The oversized clothing I had donated during *#projectloseweight* were desperately needed again.

Months later, I saw Dr. Foley. I'll never forget how I felt as I sat in his waiting room, knowing I was at my breaking point. I was bigger than I was the first time I saw him. He told me I needed to consider a more permanent solution and that I'd be an excellent candidate for gastric bypass surgery. He had enough documentation on me, so he'd be able to verify to the insurance company that the procedure was medically necessary. Despite our best efforts, though, my insurance did not cover the procedure. They considered it a luxury. So… life continued, my size swelled and my best attempts failed. However, as a notable meme goes… *Nevertheless, she persisted.*

In December 2016, I was selected for a promotion at work. I remember panicking ahead of the interview, knowing full well I needed to wear a blazer and did not have one that fit. My husband and I spent hours scouring the town's resale shops, thrift stores and the very limited plus-size clothing stores. I had two days from the notification to the actual interview. I found a collarless jacket that I hoped the executive team would see as an effort to look the part. Thankfully, I was successful and was promoted from a director to a chief. I remember coming home to celebrate and telling my husband what I was going to do with those extra earnings. I was finally going to invest in *myself.*

I took out a personal loan and invested around $20,000 for gastric sleeve surgery. I only told the people who needed to know until after the surgery was done. I knew I would face humiliation and shame for taking the easy way out because most people didn't know my whole story. That concern was justified when I was told by one of them that they knew of people who had done that and gained it all back.

The Hands They Were Dealt

On January 18, 2018, I found myself on a gurney. I was about to permanently alter my body after going through months of pre-surgical requirements such as nutritionists and psychiatric evaluations. I was terrified. I had stepped on the scale that morning and witnessed the highest numbers I had ever seen staring up at me:

465 pounds.

My terror leveled up as I thought about that number. Would I wake up from surgery? What if I failed at this, too, and what would I do and say about it? I chose to focus on two things that really drove me to that point. First, I wanted to someday have a child. Second, I wanted to call myself a runner. Those were my motivations.

It was the first time I had spent the night in a hospital. I remember being in terrible pain, poked and prodded, and woken up every hour despite being utterly exhausted. After meeting the necessary milestones to be released, I was finally on the road home. The short 15-minute drive home was very bumpy and caused extreme nausea. The combination of being car-sick and having post-surgical stomach sensitivity produced the eruptive results one would expect. In that moment, I thought of all those "easy way out" comments that came from a place of zero knowledge or empathy. Nothing in the first few weeks was easy. I was in constant pain and only able to eat teaspoon-sized amounts of food while my stomach healed.

I began to lose more and more pounds but was restricted to no more than 1/4-cup of food per meal for the first few months. I was also told to get up and move as much as possible. Friends would come over and walk with me around my cul-de-sac. I remember feeling exhausted, and I had pain beyond the surgical pain because my body couldn't handle a 1/4-mile walk. My feet were on fire, I had shin split pain, and my lower back ached so badly because I still carried a good deal of weight.

Thankfully, in three months, I lost my first 100 pounds. The freedoms

I started to see were intoxicating. I could fit into a stadium seat at Pikes Peak Center and Ball Arena. I could sit without anxiety in a booth at a restaurant.

In January 2019, a year after my surgery, I noted a few of my proudest non-scale victories. They may not mean much to an average-sized person, but they were life-giving to me:

- Comfortably wearing a seatbelt
- Buying clothes off the rack in the women's section
- Crossing my legs while sitting
- Wearing wedge shoes
- Touching my toes and tying my shoes
- Riding a rollercoaster
- Four tighter notches on my watch band
- Flying comfortably on a plane without a seat belt extender
- Wedding ring was resized
- Easily shaving my legs
- Mowing the lawn
- Going from size 12 shoe size to size 10
- Standing for longer than ten minutes
- No longer needing oxygen at night and no more sleep apnea
- My husband wrapping his arms entirely around me in a hug

That same month, I decided to work on one of my goals and train myself to be a runner. I set my sights on the Bolder Boulder, an annual 10k Memorial Day weekend run which falls around my birthday. It felt right to celebrate my 35th birthday by running 6.2 miles with 50,000 people.

Every morning leading up to race day, I'd wake up and walk or run, depending on the self-guided *Couch to 10k* app I was following. During those early morning walks, I had great moments of reflection and beaming pride. I was still losing weight and blessing my body with movement. I was accomplishing my goal of calling myself a runner.

The Hands They Were Dealt

I promised myself one thing about the Bolder Boulder: I would run the entire race. Actually, I would *jog* the entire race. I would keep moving and not stop. I would *not* walk like I did all those times at track practice or during volleyball tryouts. The only thing I wanted from the event was to cross that finish line, to feel the victory of accomplishing a goal and to finally call myself a runner. On race day, I weighed in at my lightest recorded weight since my weight loss journey began: 247 pounds.

I did it. I didn't stop.

Life took a hard turn in October 2020. After years of trying to conceive with my husband, we learned we had substantial infertility issues. My fallopian tubes were blocked, and the risk of an ectopic pregnancy was extremely high. The only way a child was possible in my body would be through invitro fertilization (IVF). I was still paying on the personal loan I took out for my weight loss surgery. The thought of taking out another loan with an entry-level price tag of $25,000-$30,000 was financially overwhelming. Bearing a child would not be in the cards for me, after all.

That realization hit hard in the first few weeks. I recalled the euphoria of crossing the finish line at the Bolder Bolder and accomplishing that goal, and I knew this goal would never be fulfilled. There were many tears shed. The holiday season that year was particularly difficult thinking about sentimental family moments we'd never have.

The hits kept coming. In January 2021, my husband and I decided our marriage was not something we wanted to continue. My life was on a dark path of divorce that I could never have imagined. It was also the best thing that ever happened to me. I sold my house, paid off the first surgery debt and decided to invest in myself yet again.

One of the most unspoken consequences about extreme weight loss is the amount of excessive loose skin. I had lost just over 200 pounds. There comes a point where skin just doesn't tighten up from that. While clothed, much of my appearance was dramatically improved, and I had a *much* higher degree of confidence, but when I saw myself naked I absolutely hated me. Yes… hated.

I had worked so hard and gone through the ringer. I endured physical agony and went to emotional hell and back, and I still saw 465-pound Shannon. Despite what anyone else said, that's what I saw. Those *Shannon, you're beautiful, sexy, gorgeous, stunning, radiant* compliments would never resonate with me as long as I saw myself in the mirror with pounds and pounds of leftover skin hanging there.

The post-divorce sale of my house allowed me to consider yet another financial decision. Could I make one more investment in myself to finally rid myself of "465 Shannon" and let her *feel* like the 200-pound-lesser person she is? The answer was yes.

On January 12, 2022, nearly four years to the day after my gastric surgery, I went under the knife in the capable hands of Dr. Kamran Dastoury. Doctors and nurses took pictures and marked up my naked body as I stood there. That level of vulnerability was a fearful experience, but the team was exceptional and made me feel comfortable in all my glory.

The medical professionals at Modern Surgical Arts interact with many patients, but one nurse in particular, Catherine, said something to me I'll never forget. She thanked me for getting her energized in her work because she felt like helping me was truly *functional* medicine. She was eager to put their skills to work by helping me become free from my previous body. Sixteen pounds of excess skin were removed from my mid-section; it was an extreme tummy tuck. In that moment, I knew this surgery was really going to change my life.

In the days that followed, the nausea and pain I experienced during my first surgery felt like a vacation compared to this. There are no words to describe the agony of the first 24 hours. I would not have been able to survive those hours, or any of the following days and weeks, without the help of my best friend, Mary. She gracefully cleaned my incisions, filled my water, injected me with medication, carefully laid out every pill I needed to take, gave my dog belly rubs, and even had her husband come over and cook for me.

Ahead of that surgery, I had snagged a dress on an epic Black Friday deal. I would not have been able to pull that off in my pre-surgery body, but I hoped I would rock the hell out of that thing post-surgery. If you reference the picture at the start of this chapter, you will see that dress.

As I donned that dress three weeks after my skin surgery, I literally collapsed in sheer bliss because it fit beautifully. In that moment, all the hard work, pain, agony, shame, regret and feelings of unworthiness over the last 30 years of my life washed away.

When I put on that dress, I realized I was entirely in charge of loving myself. I understood, finally and for myself, that I was—am—beautiful.

I am resilient.

I am a fighter.

I have developed and discovered my style and my self-worth. I proudly own over 60 blazers. I have a sneaker collection that gives me confidence to lean into my true self and flex my unique style. I wear sequins because *It's a Tuesday, and why not.* I could now confidently pull off all the styles I wanted to previously when I was relegated to dressing like a grandma.

I have done much internal work and reflection with the support of my therapist. That girl who pulled the peanut butter dough from the trash is no longer who I am. I am not the cheater who faked running laps around the track. I have learned a great deal from those experiences, mostly that they—along with numbers on the scale—do not define me.

I hope you can take something away from my story. If nothing else, know this: You are in charge of you. You must speak up. You must advocate for yourself. You must believe in *you* first. No one else can do it for you.

You, like me, have 465 reasons to smile and radiate your light into this world. Happiness and joy look good on you.

Shannon Coker is the Chief Operating Officer at Care and Share Food Bank for Southern Colorado, boasting an impressive 16-year tenure with the organization. In her current role, she orchestrates the seamless operation of partner agencies, programs and direct service initiatives, extending her oversight to distribution centers in Colorado Springs, Pueblo and the San Luis Valley. Shannon skillfully manages the transportation fleet, food procurement and volunteers, showcasing her multifaceted leadership. With a remarkable journey encompassing seven different positions within Care and Share, her unwavering dedication to the organization is evident.

Beyond her professional commitments, Shannon extends her impact as a board member at the Humane Society of the Pikes Peak Region. A versatile talent, she channels her artistic side as a photographer, specializing in capturing the essence of families and children. Shannon hands often get muddy indulging in the therapeutic art of pottery. Her heart belongs to Nile, her 8-year-old pit bull, whom she affectionately rubs the belly of, creating a perfect harmony between her professional prowess and personal passions.

The Hands They Were Dealt

IN THE DANCE OF LIFE, RESILIENCE IS
THE CHOREOGRAPHY THAT TRANSFORMS
STUMBLING BLOCKS INTO STEPPING STONES. IT'S
THE ART OF DEFYING THE ODDS, WHERE EVERY
FALL BECOMES A CHANCE TO RISE, AND EVERY
CHALLENGE SHAPES THE RHYTHM OF TRIUMPH.

CHAPTER FOUR

Breaking Away: Triumph Over Physical Abuse

Sadie Solstice

When I was eighteen years old and pregnant, I found myself in a unique situation. I became a victim of domestic abuse. Marlon, my abuser and the father of my child, had been my friend since middle school. We'd had a brief romantic relationship and remained close friends. He was able to attract people with his charisma, but he would also repel them with his lack of respect and selfishness. I felt sorry for the poor girls who found themselves under his manipulation. At the time, it was light-hearted; and I would usually laugh about it. We were in high school after all, and I didn't yet understand the gravity of his narcissism.

When I entered my senior year, he and I became very close. I thought I saw a change in him. He was kinder. He dreamed big, he liked to help people, and he wanted to make an impact. Like many teenage girls, I had low self-esteem. I saw him in a bright shining light that told me he was better than me. I fell in love with his charm, the persona he put on to impress everyone around him. He was hilarious and goofy, but intelligent and spiritual at the same time. During my spring break, we went for a road trip into the mountains and had a crazy adventure during which I discovered my love for him. On this vacation, he convinced me to try LSD with him. After that, my world changed. It all felt very positive.

After graduating high school, we traveled together more often. He didn't feel the same way about me that I did for him, though. We had always said we were best friends and not dating; but after a summer of agony in my unrequited love, we made our relationship official. We had been staying with friends and also at our parents' homes from time to time. My family had eventually lost respect for Marlon, and I was making poor choices as I followed his lead. I found myself bouncing back and forth between my mom's place and my dad's, and I slept in my car most nights. During this period, Marlon convinced me it would be a fantastic idea to get pregnant. He said it would be a way to bond ourselves forever. We could raise a child to be confident, spiritual and capable of anything. It didn't faze us that we had no money and nowhere to live.

On February 5th, 2017, a friend of ours asked us to bring him some groceries because he was without a car. After spending a little time with that friend, Marlon asked him if he had any acid. He gave Marlon a few drops from a vial, then we left. I wanted to drop him off at his mom's house and go home to my dad's (where Marlon wasn't allowed), but he asked me to stay with him so he wouldn't have to trip at home with his family. We sat in the car outside his house. Pregnant and exhausted, I laid back to get some rest.

A few hours later, I woke up extremely thirsty and feeling nauseous. We went to a Denny's to get water and toast. On the way there, I asked him how he was feeling. He replied that the acid hadn't hit him yet. Marlon used LSD so often that he'd built up a tolerance to it, so this didn't surprise me. However, I noticed him acting in strange ways. After leaving Denny's, I decided we could probably stay in the car for a couple more hours. Once my dad left for work in the morning, we could just hang out at his house. We drove to his parent's house and sat there once again to wait. I rested my eyes to get more rest.

I awoke to a freezing cold hand grabbing my leg. "We need to hide!" he said. Confused and noticing Marlon's heavy breathing and panicked expression, I asked him what we needed to hide from. "I'm not sure, but we need to hide. You're God, right?" As many times as I had tripped with or sat with him, I'd never seen Marlon act this way. I figured the solution to this was to take him somewhere safe, hoping he would wake up soon and be back to his usual self. We drove to my dad's house while Marlon sang off-beat and off-key to a song on the radio. I laughed at him, but I also worried about this weird behavior.

When we got to my dad's place, I got both of us undressed and into bed. I was deliriously tired, and Marlon kept talking nonsense to me. "Is it water?" he asked me over and over again. I ignored him, hoping he would fall asleep soon. That's when he got on top of me.

I was able to kick him off me after his attempt to sexually assault me. I angrily stormed off into my dad's bedroom and locked myself in the bathroom. Marlon followed behind me, jiggling the handle and banging on the door. I yelled at him to leave me alone and heard him run down the stairs, making a ruckus. Concerned, I went down to check on him and found him in the garage digging through my dad's tools. He had a hammer in his hands. I was able to wrestle it away from him, genuinely scared now of whatever was happening.

He ran upstairs and I put the hammer away, then I followed him. Through the partially open door, I saw Marlon giggling and splashing in the bathroom sink. I pushed the door open and asked him what was going on. His fist met my face as he shouted, "No! You can't come in!" I fell back onto the floor in the hallway, stunned. He slammed the door shut, and I retreated into the guest room to the right. This room didn't have a lock, so I leaned up against the door and asked myself who I could call for help. *I can forgive him for hitting me. After all, he's on drugs and not in his right mind.*

I didn't want to call the police and get Marlon into trouble, so I called a friend whom I knew had a car. My friend didn't answer his phone, so I sent him a text message: *Marlon is beating me. I'm at my dad's. Please come help me!* Before I could get a response, Marlon barged his way into the

The Hands They Were Dealt

guest room. He tossed my phone to the floor and lifted me onto the bed.

"Pain isn't even real," he said before biting my bottom lip with all his force. I screamed in pain, hoping my dog downstairs might hear me. While again attempting to sexually assault me, he hit me and bit me more. My phone's alarm clock was going off in the corner, which scared him. I told him that if he let me up I could turn it off, and he agreed. "Is it water?" he asked me again.

"Yes, Marlon, yes. It's water. Stay here. I'll go get you some water right now." I fled down the stairs and spotted my dog in the living room. Marlon followed behind me, and I sicked my dog onto him. "Get him, Trixie! Get him!" She jumped on him, barking as I ran out of the house into the garage and into my car. *My keys are inside!* I hurried back in and grabbed my jacket with the key fob in the pocket. I saw Marlon petting Trixie and trying to calm her.

I ran back out, but he followed me and opened the passenger door to the car. "No, no," he said. "I'm getting you water, remember? Stay here." Then he urinated in my car. I backed away, shocked and horrified, as he laughed and chased me around with his running stream. I ran across the cul-de-sac to my neighbor, Starla. She noticed me waving frantically at her, and motioned to me that she was going to call 911.

Suddenly, Marlon picked me up and pulled me back into the house, leaving the garage door open. "I know what I need to do," he said. "I need to kill you." His hands were around my throat, I was laying on the floor as he towered above me. I was kicking and trying to fight him off me. Then everything went black. When I came to, he was on top of me again. He had grabbed a kitchen knife from the butcher block on the counter.

I have almost no recollection of the events that followed. I was later informed by neighbors and police about what happened. Trixie had run outside while Marlon was choking me. She would normally run to our neighbor's house to play with their dog, but she didn't this time. She ran to Tim's house, barking at his door until he came out. He saw our open garage and walked Trixie back in, where he saw me being stabbed by Marlon. Tim's appearance distracted Marlon enough for me to get up and run out the back door.

Marlon ran at Tim with his knife in hand. Tim slammed the door in Marlon's face, then made sure I was okay outside. He came back in, grabbed Marlon and threw him up against the wall. He banged his hand on the wall until Marlon dropped the knife. By this time, the entire neighborhood was wondering what was happening and had called my dad. My neighbor, John, rushed to my house to assist Tim in holding Marlon down while they waited for the police. I was waiting for an ambulance at Judy's and not fully certain what had happened to me.

Marlon stabbed me thirteen times—twice in my abdomen, once in the neck, twice in my arm, three times on my leg and five times in my back. I had defensive wounds on my fingers, my face was bruised and swollen, my eyes were black, and the vessels in one eye had burst. My left lung collapsed, and I needed a blood transfusion. Despite all these injuries, my unborn baby was unharmed. I stayed in the hospital with my family for three days and went home to my mom's house afterward so she could take care of me.

I could hardly walk. I couldn't use my hands much because they were bandaged up, and I was supposed to rest as much as possible. Marlon was arrested after being taken to the hospital; he had stabbed himself in the leg during my assault. He took a plea deal but was ultimately convicted. His was initially charged with two attempted murders (against Tim and me), three assault charges, two attempted sexual assaults, menacing with a deadly weapon, obstruction of telephone service, and kidnapping. His plea deal consisted of fictitious charges to get the range of sentencing that the DA and public defender agreed to. He was sentenced to 13 years with time served during the 2-year court process.

I stayed with Marlon for those two years, advocating for my own

The Hands They Were Dealt

attacker. I was a scared, single teen mother who didn't want to let go of the person I had manufactured in my head. The person I loved so dearly wasn't real; he was someone I had idolized and created in place of the physical person. This was how I coped with betrayal from my best friend whom I had loved and imagined building a life with. I finally found the courage to leave him after realizing I was spending 12 cents per minute to speak with him on the phone. All he did in those conversations was put me down and make me feel bad about myself. Why did I let this man—who tried to kill me and showed no remorse—make me feel inferior to him? I was a brave, optimistic, bright, fun and intelligent woman. I'm a good mother, and I love to help others. I didn't deserve anything I had gone through with him.

I deserved a life of prosperity, abundance, adventure and love. After facing my death, I learned a very real truth: we all die. Every one of us will die, and it can happen at any moment. I almost died at 18, very young and healthy. Death doesn't discriminate; it comes for us all. Why not live like there's no tomorrow? Why waste any time on this Earth? I look at Earth as if I were a tourist. One wouldn't visit Paris without viewing the Eiffel Tower, so why visit Earth without seeing the ocean or the pyramids? Why live without trying zip lining, camping, rock climbing, shark diving, whale watching, skydiving, swimming, scuba diving, snorkeling… you get the idea.

With the help of my friends, family and the brand I created, Get Life, I have been able to check off many bucket list items with many more to go. I've been to Cairo, Egypt, and I've seen the pyramids of Giza. I've taken my son to Disney World to meet Mickey Mouse for his fourth birthday. I've gone swimming with dolphins. I've been skydiving. I've traveled all over the United States and have left the country many times. I have so many more things to do, and at every opportunity I invite people to come with me.

It would have been easy to regard my situation with self-pity, and I often did. People wouldn't have blamed me for giving up on happiness and love after hearing my story. I see every event in my life as an opportunity to become more of who I truly am. When we are born, we forget who we were. Our souls know us through eternity, but our human minds forget. Earth is a chance to learn about yourself and find meaning.

The events that took place on the morning of February 6, 2017, gave me a beautiful opportunity. Would I be resentful, unforgiving, fun-hating, boring and lifeless; or would I be resilient, brave, fun-loving, adventurous and alive? My positive mindset won't undo the damage the trauma has done, and I still have nightmares. I fear that Marlon, when released from prison, will try to find my son and me. My body still doesn't trust people, and my mental health could always use some improvement. Yet, I wouldn't go back in time to change anything.

Under Marlon's thumb, I never would have stepped up into a leadership position. I wouldn't have met my current partner and built the business and career that I have. I wouldn't have been able to make an impact on others the way I do now. If my story gets just one person to say, "I will live life today, I will not wait, I will chase my dreams with reckless abandon, I will check off my bucket list, I will love fully, and I will prosper," that will make every moment worthwhile for me.

Humans have two true motivations in life: the avoidance of pain and the gaining of pleasure. The former is stronger than the latter. Humans don't always give their all to gain pleasure; otherwise, everyone would live their dream lives. But they will do anything and everything to avoid pain. For me, the pain of never doing all I want to do on Earth before death comes to collect me is an excruciating possibility I will work hard to avoid. I'll do anything to ensure I've visited every city I want to visit and done every activity I want to do. I want to help my son and others do the same.

Find a pain that's worth avoiding and use it to motivate yourself to live for *you*. I'm thankful for the trauma I endured and the hope and motivation it's given me.

The Hands They Were Dealt

Sadie Solstice is a Denver native and proud mother to an inspiring little boy who fuels her quest to be the best version of herself. As the founder of Get Life, a brand dedicated to promoting intentional living, she orchestrates fundraising events, community activities and global journeys that encourage people to design their lives. Through Get Life training and memoirs, she has also embraced public speaking, sharing her story to inspire others.

Join Sadie on her empowering journey by creating meaningful connections and crafting lives filled with purpose and adventure.

Sadie's passion extends to social media, where she can be found on Facebook, Instagram, and TikTok under the username LilMissS80.

CHAPTER FIVE

Choose to L;VE

Alicia Nolan

I knew five minutes before arriving at my house what I would find.

I knew I'd find notes. I knew my gun would be missing. I knew my wife was gone. It was our extreme connection and the series of events that had taken place throughout the morning that told me my entire life had been turned upside down. As I was on the phone with 911 to report my wife missing, a sheriff's deputy was at my door. *Wow, that was really fast,* I thought. He borrowed my phone and went outside while he spoke to the 911 operator still on the line. When he came back in, he asked me to sit down. He told me he was sorry to have to notify me that they found my wife that morning. She was gone.

I immediately fell to the ground and cried harder than I thought possible. She was really gone. I never thought I'd experience the reality of being a widow whose wife died by suicide. It was something that could not be undone and that would never go away. The human being to whom I was so connected felt like she would be better off dead than battling her demons, and I would have to live with that fact. I never would have expected this outcome regardless of what anyone said.

We were about to turn a new page to our future, and things were looking up. We had planned that weekend to take a long bath together and spend some quality time. The following weekend was her birthday, and a week after that we were to attend a concert. We had plans to travel over-

The Hands They Were Dealt

seas and to return to Greece where we had our honeymoon. We had plans to buy a plot of land and downsize for our dream home. We had plans to grow old together playing board games, hiking and doing all the things we loved to do together. It was all gone now. I never thought my wife would leave me, let alone in this manner. We used to joke that one of us would be gone shortly after something horrible happened to the other because we couldn't live without each other. The very thought of living without the other was so incredibly terrifying that we would not want to live on. My nightmare came true.

Many different factors led to this horrific event; mental health was the biggest of them all. I wish my wife would have noticed the patterns I had seen in the months leading up to this. I wish she would have had the self-awareness to see that some of her behaviors were abnormal. I wish I could have done more to help her see it, as well.

About three months earlier, I had come to the conclusion that my wife was suffering from borderline personality disorder. I immediately signed up for related Facebook groups and started reading books about the condition. I knew she wouldn't be receptive about it, so I did research, changed the way I addressed certain topics and made sure to validate her feelings no matter what. This approach was working with her, but I just couldn't dig her out of her recent low point. Her demons took over and there was nothing I could do.

There were major events which deeply affected my wife prior to her suicide. I was away at work and unable to help her with them. She also had an unhealthy decades-old relationship with Ambien and had started vaping marijuana and taking ADHD medications within six months of ending her life. I believe all of this was to mask what was really going on inside. In the end, it kept her from thinking clearly, if at all.

It may seem common that I should blame myself (some of you may be thinking that) for not being more aggressive with helping her or even trying to get her admitted to a hospital; but I really did do everything I could to help her. Mental health is evil, and it shows its face in so many different forms. I never thought she would ever take her life. All I can do with her story is to encourage people to talk and get help if they find themselves leaning toward suicide. Please get help. Think about the people who love you and care for you, because it really does have a lasting impact on them.

I would like to get into my journey and face the daily battle I have fought ever since then. I want to keep going and build a new normal. My own mental health has suffered greatly, and I have done my absolute best to keep fighting and to find tools to help me with my battle from day one.

After being told about my wife, I made phone calls to family and friends, and they came over immediately. I have the best support system and crew of people that anyone could ever ask for. A buddy from the National Guard was the first person to arrive within 20 minutes of being informed. He asked what he could do, and I told him to take all the alcohol out of the house. I had not consumed alcohol since November 27, 2020, and I knew what would happen if any of it stayed in the house. This was certainly the type of event that would send me back into my old ways, and I knew I couldn't do that to myself or anyone who cared about me.

I remain sober to this day. This was the first of many decisions I would make based on my own self-awareness to keep from self-destructing. People started filtering into the house over the next few days and reaching out every day. Every amazing person in my life asked what they could do, and I gave only one request every time: I did not want to be alone. For the first month, I had someone with me 24/7. Friends and family stayed overnight at my house and took shifts to make sure I wasn't alone.

I don't know if I ever explained to them why I didn't want to be alone, but people around me are so amazing that they didn't need to understand. They just made sure my request was fulfilled. Those people will never fully understand what they did for me. Darkness had crept in and festered within my mental state, and I did not know where to go. I didn't know what to do or where to go from there, but I knew that at some point I needed to embrace the loneliness. At some point, people need to get back to their lives, and I needed to attempt to get used to my new normal.

The depression and anxiety were deep. Panic attacks caught me off guard at all times of the day. My only reason for getting up in the morning was to feed the three cats we had gotten together. I had also been diagnosed with a form of PTSD, so I decided to get a service dog. I rescued her from an unfavorable living situation where someone was using her to breed. She's an amazing French bulldog who I named Juna, which means "new moon" or "new beginning." She has been my rock and the reason why I keep going. At the beginning I needed a reason, and she came into my life at the perfect time. She goes everywhere with me—on airplanes, on long road trips—and is the best companion I could ever ask for. It's as if she was born to be my companion.

I have faced some of the darkest days of my life since August 17, 2022. One of the hardest things to withstand is the fogginess and lack of mental function. I don't have the memory I used to have, and I'm not as sharp as I used to be. It's one of the most frustrating changes because I feel inadequate. I feel stupid at times because I can't get my stuff together, but it's also something I'm learning to adapt to. I make more lists now and must ensure I put everything in my calendar in order to remember my schedule.

I still have days of emotional and physical heaviness I can't shake. I try to force myself to get up and move around, but I quite literally can't. I just have to listen to what my body is telling me and rest. This can be difficult with many projects on your plate, but I manage and still get stuff done.

This is MY healing journey. It's not for anyone else to decide whether it's the right or wrong way to heal. There is no right way to heal, and I want everyone who reads this to remember that. No matter what life throws at you, whatever the event may be, it is up to you to decide what is right and healthy for you. I'm telling you this for a reason. You are going to hear things like *You need to wait a year to do this*, or *It's too soon to do that*, but that is up to you to decide and no one else. Also keep in mind that people mean well and have good intentions. Those kinds of comments come from a place of love, and it's okay to tell people that you will do what you think is right for yourself.

Part of my healing journey involved meeting another wonderful human being. Most people think it was too early for that. Believe me, I was my own devil's advocate, and I questioned the feelings I was having; but I can't ignore the fact that this person is so fantastic and that we are capable of having hard conversations. The connection we have is undeniable. We have both questioned if this was the right thing to do, but there is no such thing as "right" for anyone.

I still suffer from anxiety and PTSD, and depression wears me down at times. She is the most open and supportive person anyone could have by their side after such a horrible tragedy. I never thought I could love so deeply again. It's a deeper love than I could have ever imagined, and I'm so grateful. We help each other with our healing, and we support each other by creating a safe environment of communication and openness.

One of the most important parts of my journey is what I have chosen to do with my pain and trauma. I have a dual master's degree in Homeland Security/Emergency Disaster Management and a bachelor's degree in criminal justice. However, I chose my true passion by becoming a certified personal trainer and helping others with their health and fitness journey. I had been doing personal training for a while, but there was always a possibility of leaving that to take on federal opportunities. At the end of the day, helping others with their health and fitness journey is truly what I need and is something I thoroughly enjoy.

I've also learned about bridging the mind-body connection to give others a more wholesome approach to fitness. The mind-body connection

The Hands They Were Dealt

is powerful. The mental and emotional side of physical fitness cannot be ignored and must be worked on together as a unit. I love talking to people about mental health and being able to just listen.

Another important project I accomplished was creating and trade-marking a brand called L;VE. A portion of those proceeds goes to Pikes Peak Suicide Prevention Partnership (PPSPP) located in Colorado. I have a strong, emotional desire to give back to a struggling community, and I cannot help but feed into that pull. The semicolon in the brand represents those who have struggled with thoughts of suicide. Its meaning is derived from its use in writing where it represents an intention to keep going and continue a story. My brand is designed to inspire others to keep going, whether for themselves or for a passerby who sees it. I want to remind people to keep fighting and that they are loved. I do not want other families and friends to feel the same pain I have felt.

There is so much healing in helping others, and that is what I have chosen to do with my journey. The conversations I have had with people at vendor events and expos have been so eye opening and comforting. To look a stranger in the eyes and become familiar with a similar pain is powerful. Conversations are imperative to the connection we have with others.

I encourage everyone to have those hard conversations. Be open with each other. There is no shame in the feelings you have. Whether telling your story to a family member or a complete stranger, there is much strength in opening up and sharing whatever may be pressing on your mind.

Also, be candid. Not everyone is a great listener. You are allowed to preface your feelings of expression with *I don't need advice,* or *I just need you to listen.* At times, people may be inclined to say they know how you feel, and that can be detrimental to our expression. But please don't give up.

I never thought I would be a widow. I never thought I would feel the pain and heartbreak I have felt. I never thought I would be where I am today. My life was supposed to be very different, and it flipped on its head in a matter of seconds. But I am fighting. I have chosen to take my healing journey and do something positive with it for others.

I hope that my story inspires others to do the same. I hope my story inspires others to keep fighting for themselves and every single person who cares about them. I also want my story to inspire others to be kind and to just love each other. There is too much hate in this world. We are all human beings and make mistakes. It is what you do with those mistakes and the choices you make that can make a great impact. Choose to live. Choose to love. Choose to be kind.

Alicia Nolan is the visionary owner of Choose to L;VE, LLC in Colorado, which passionately champions suicide prevention and mental health awareness. Her company, driven by a commitment to change, produces impactful apparel and products under the trademarked brand *L;VE*, with a significant portion of sales contributing to the Pikes Peak Suicide Prevention Partnership in Colorado Springs. Recognized for her advocacy, Alicia had the honor of being interviewed on *BCC Evolution (S8:E1)*, a segment broadcasted on various platforms.

Alicia invites you to join her in fostering awareness, compassion, and support for mental health, making a tangible impact in the realm of suicide prevention.

To delve deeper into her mission and initiatives, explore Alicia's website at www.choosetolive.org. Connect with her on Facebook at facebook.com/hnflve or reach out via email at owner@choosetolive.org.

CHAPTER SIX

The Third-Culture Kid

Rozen Lalas

I'm the girl who looks like I have it *made*. I've lived in Los Angeles for 10 years. I've got the car, the off-white little fluffy dog, the high-rise ceilings in an all-white apartment with a palm tree view, and some days I can wear sweatpants to work in my living room and be on set directing talent other days. Annoying, right?

I make a living by helping people, brands and companies share their stories. I am a full-time content producer. When you scroll through social media and see an ad that stimulates you to purchase a random foundation product, that's from me. I am also a content creator for my freelance business where I help others through compelling social media content. I tell stories of young moms struggling with under-eye circles and work with influencers to lead her audience as she transitions from actress to breathwork instructor. I've been helping people tell their stories for over two years. I'm really great at it, and I actually love it.

Something feels very different about this current season, though. I realize I've never told *my* story. Content producing takes up around 2-8 hours a day, 5 days a week. Between work, I create as an independent Pop/R&B artist. I tell my story in the nuances of my songs, but I've never sat down and written it all out. Funny how this is all taking place at the same time. This realization is hitting me at a divine moment exactly one week away from releasing my debut album. I'm finally writing *my* story here in my brand-new LA apartment. I can't help but feel like I've been waiting in line forever to audition, and now they're finally calling, yelling my name to the stage.

I look like a typical, trendy, creative Millennial living in Los Angeles until you ask, "Who are you? Where are you from?" It's not a simple answer. I'm the person whose story is about to be the best distraction from your present life over the course of these dazzling pages. Allow me to shuffle through the cards I was dealt over my 33 years of life on this Earth. It's not a typical story, but it's a unique one. Sure, that's what everyone says; but how many people do you know who have lived in several different countries before the age of 16? How many third-culture kids do you personally know? Wikipedia states:

> "Third culture kids (TCK), or third culture individuals (TCI),
> are people who were raised in a culture other than their parents'
> or the culture of their country of nationality, and who also live
> in a different environment during a significant part of their child
> development years. They typically are exposed to a greater volume
> and variety of cultural influences than those who grow up in one
> particular cultural setting."

Growing up as a TCK, I had the best experiences. I went to the best schools and moved from country to country every 1-4 years. We went on vacation four times a year. My core memories are from Rio de Janeiro, Brazil, running up the steps of Christ the Redeemer. That epic view rendered my little lungs absolutely breathless. I remember running along the shore of the beach with my sister and seeing women wearing very uncomfortable and revealing little thongs. I had never seen those before.

I miss how my father used to remind me of my first Eiffel Tower visit. I was so tired from walking my 5-year-old legs through the streets of Paris. By the time we got to the tower, I was throwing a full-on fit. One of my favorite childhood memories is our trip to London. I remember I was so happy to take a photo of me figuratively chopping of my brother's head in the London Dungeon after we "made it out alive." I remember accidentally drooling on my dad's shoulder while he carried me through the dungeon because I was so scared. The one that really took the cake, though, was the Taj Mahal trip. Our whole family, including our driver, Gitender, was caught in the rain on the side of the road in a broken-down Tata Sumo with a busted headlight while returning from the Taj Mahal. *How did I get born into this life?*

Life is one big game, and I hit the jackpot with the deck of cards I was handed. My playground spanned the globe—Africa, India, Thailand, England—before I hit sweet sixteen. Sounds like something out of a fairy tale, right? Here's the deal, though: luxury doesn't always guarantee "happily ever after."

We had fancy schools, personal chauffeurs and a magic wand of a maid who would fold, press and arrange our clothes like they were royalty. Yet, beneath all the sparkle was a hint of solitude. Traveling the world and moving from place to place every year might sound like a whirlwind adventure, but it got pretty darn lonely. A sense of belonging was more elusive than a unicorn. There was never one place to call home and no familiar faces to revisit, because my family was always on the move.

Fast forward to adulthood. All those long-distance relationships I had can be blamed on the "apple doesn't fall far from the tree" phenomenon. My dad jet-setted for Coca Cola, leaving us with Mom and the adventure of a new country. It's no wonder I developed an itch to move and to put down roots somewhere fresh. Breakups hit harder. We said goodbye to friends and waved hello to new chapters. My friendships grew wings and fluttered away every time we packed our bags. But hey, I'm not complaining. I've staked my claim in the City of Angels for a solid decade now. I can finally call a place my own. The moment I graduated from Western

Michigan University, I jumped on a plane, landed at LAX and dove head-first into the rollercoaster ride of LA living.

Moving here was like a walk in the park for me. Folks back home were astonished at how I simply shrugged, grabbed my wallet with $60 in cash and boarded a plane. I was confident. Blame it on my nomadic upbringing. Whether Michigan or Madagascar, I've had an unwavering belief that I could conquer any corner of the world. That same boldness empowered me on the first day of every new school. It was game time with new faces and new places, and I became a pro at it.

Making friends was child's play. Introducing myself was second nature. I nailed it at being the center of attention. All I ever wanted was to fit in and to blend seamlessly, to become part of the scenery. But at 33, I'm embracing a new truth. I wasn't born to fit in; I was made to stand out. So, here's to embracing the quirks, celebrating the uniqueness and taking center stage in the grand theater of life. How am I doing? Do I sound confident? Well, I wasn't always this confident.

It all began when Ronnie met Zenaida. My dad was a self-made man who worked his way up from an entry-level position at Coca-Cola all the way up to a regional director. His favorite quote to me was, "Life is what you make it." When I complained about something, he would recite that with a sigh and a smile. I understand now why that quote was his favorite. Dad swooped my mom off her feet with his charm, quick wit, Jimmy Hendrix guitar skills and an unforgettable voice that captivated anyone in the room. She was the stay-at-home mom, and he was the provider.

I was born in General Santos City, Philippines, on September 4th, 1989. I showed up in the world and crashed my sister's third birthday. When I was 3 years old, my dad came home from work, crouched down to me and said, "From now on, no matter what I say, you're going to respond in English. We're moving to Africa!" I couldn't even *say* "Africa" at the time, but I knew it was a big moment because the whole house was stirring. My mom was also very loud and animated, as usual. We never knew where we were moving next. We just supported our dad and went with him wherever Coca-Cola assigned him. We constantly moved and traveled four times a year per my dad's contract. Not too shabby, right?

Through my first and second grade, we were living in Mumbai, and I was attending the American School of Bombay. By third grade, we were living in New Delhi in the most magical house. I called it The White House because we had a rose garden, a vegetable garden, a tennis court and a pool. I remember lots of marble and more rooms than I could count. I remember dramatically re-enacting the *It's All Coming Back to Me Now* music video by Celine Dion in the halls of our White House. Like I said, it was magical. We had a Dachshund named Dude, and our happy family of six lived without cable. The best thing our dad ever did for us growing up was opting out of cable TV. "If you want to watch something, you guys can watch whatever we have on VHS. I want you to enjoy the outdoors. Play outside!" It added to the magic of it all.

As I started fourth grade, we moved to Bangkok, Thailand. I remember stepping outside of the Suvarnabhumi International Airport and saying, "Dad! Are those skyscrapers?" We had a fully furnished 3-story condo overlooking a private lake on the top floor of the building. All four of us kids had our own bikes. We would bike to school every day; but if we didn't want to now and then, we'd just have our driver drop us off. It was only a 15-minute bike ride or a 5-minute drive. The leasing office across the street gave *tuk-tuk* rides anywhere within the neighborhood for just 25 baht. I made it a habit to hang out with my friends after school and eat Pocky sticks before calling it a day and riding home in a *tuk-tuk*.

Thailand is known as the Land of Smiles because it really is. Everyone greets you with a smile and treats you with the utmost hospitality. My family and I fully embraced the Thai culture within those four years of calling it home. It was the longest we'd ever lived in one place. The International

School of Bangkok was, and still is, very prestigious. The campus rivaled some of the top college campuses in the US, and the environment inspired greatness in those hallowed halls.

This sounded absolutely perfect... but it wasn't.

Those experiences were and always will be near and dear to my heart. My only wish for my child-self was to have known love over anything else. Being a third-culture kid was extremely hard. The pressure to be great weighed heavily on my siblings and me. I remember taking three admissions exams just to be accepted to that school. It was so much pressure. *What if I don't get accepted? What if I don't pass? Mom and Dad would be so embarrassed to explain to their friends that their youngest doesn't get straight A's.*

I was going to school with some of the brightest minds and some of the wealthiest families. It always felt like our family had to prove we were good enough. The more talented and smart the kids were, the more bragging rights they got. I was very scared to fail. The pressure was so intense. Sometimes, I'd avoid turning in school assignments for fear that I executed them poorly or incorrectly. In my mind, I would rather not turn in *any* assignment than risk failing at what I *did* turn in. I remember having so much anxiety about showing my report card to my parents because all I wanted was to impress them and make them proud.

I didn't get good grades until my sophomore year of high school. By that time, it seemed like my family and our friends had already deemed me as talented but not smart. I was once told by a *tita* of mine that I'd never own a business, but I would be on TV. I thought that if I performed well in school my parents would reward me by buying things for me and singing my praises. If I got good grades, they'd love me more. If I performed well, I'd received love. At least, that's what I told myself.

I wish I could have been safely tended to whenever I experienced emotional turmoil. I wish I could have been held by someone during moments of weakness or hurt. I wish it would have been okay to *feel*. As physically present as my family was, no one was emotionally present for me. The only thing that was present was myself and my craft. I was just a wide-eyed, creative genius kid along for the ride.

Hello, hormones! In sixth grade, ISB's middle school department hosted an evening where moms and their daughters could learn about female hygiene. We had that awkward sex talk in health class. We teach our kids in school how to protect from STDs and how to practice safe sex, yet we do not teach them how to protect their hearts. My fragile adolescent heart was an exposed wound waiting for someone to tend to it. Having a lavish lifestyle never prepared me for the pain of adolescence and adult relationships. I was just a lonely little rich girl with no one to hold me in my misery. Since the tender age of 11, I had unknowingly looked for love in all the wrong places.

It was the age of MSN Messenger, and a boy at school caught my eye. Rake (not his real name) was a French-Canadian boy with brown hair and kind brown eyes. I didn't know it then, but by the time my hormones kicked in, I was in trouble. I felt like it was my mission in life to be loved. We did nothing more than talk on the phone every night and chat endlessly after school on Messenger. My pre-pubescent heart would skip a beat every time I'd see him log on. I just needed my person—someone to talk to and keep my thoughts and hopes and dreams safe within his embrace. I grew up with maids, drivers and people who would handle anything and everything for me, so why would I choose to do life alone? I had my first "kinda-boyfriend" at age 11. I was too young for it to go anywhere, not to mention we moved again by the end of 7th grade.

By the 8th grade, my dad was assigned back to Lagos, Nigeria. This time, it was just me and my parents; my three other siblings weren't there. My eldest brother, Carlo, had graduated from high school and was off to a university. He had his then-high school sweetheart of two years (now wife), and they were off to start their lives together as a long-distance couple. I

The Hands They Were Dealt

would not see him for a while. My next older brother, Paolo, was starting his senior year at the American Community School of Cobham, Surrey, in England. My sister, Donna, was also there with him starting her junior year. At the time, there wasn't a huge international student population in Lagos. My entire 8th-grade class consisted of less than 40 kids.

The American International School of Lagos only offered classes up to 9th grade. Because of that, my parents thought it was best to have Paolo and Donna attend ACS just six hours north by plane. We were all within the same time zone which made for easy communication, despite the hardship of long-distance parenting. I didn't realize how much I took my siblings for granted. I went from being the youngest of four kids to being the only kid in the house. I went dark. I became an "emo" kid who only wore black and navy blue, a necktie, baggy pants, dark eyeliner, spikey jewelry and heelies.

We went from a full house of six to a small party of three. I made friends right away. I remember my parents picking me up after my first day of 8th grade and laughing at the sight of me kissing my new friends farewell on the cheek like a sophisticated French woman. A lot was changing during this time of my life. I was the only child at home, we had moved again, and I also got my period. *Ta-daa!* I was officially a woman! I graduated in a sense, and so did my hormone levels.

Those hormones led me to be close to the boy across the street. Mark (not his real name) became my Rake. He was brown, and I was brown. We somehow felt safe to be each other's person behind closed doors. At school you'd think we were strangers. But on the phone, we were best friends. We spoke on the phone every night and discussed all our hopes, dreams and teenage angst, and we both had a common passion for music. I looked for love within our friendship. I felt safe, secure and supported. I wanted a Mark everywhere I went, but I could never bring him with me. Like many times before, I said goodbye to that friendship because I thought I'd never see them again. After only a year in Lagos, Nigeria, I joined my sister in England for my freshman year of high school. It was another fresh start.

In 2004, I went off to a 5-star boarding school at the fresh age of 14. By this time, it was just my sister and me. My brothers were both off to university. Carlo was still in Bangkok, and Paolo was in Wales attending there. I was so glad I had my older sister at ACS. It meant that she'd already have friends and I'd be taken care of. I remember the day I said good-bye to my mom and dad. I grew up so quickly in that very moment. It was also the year they said "I love you" to me for the first time over a phone call from my sister's dorm room. When we hung up the phone and looked at each other, it was as if both our hearts had been restored. *I know. I know they love us.* I knew it the whole time; I just needed to be told.

I should have realized then that my primary love language was Words of Affirmation, but what 14-year-old is fluent in love languages? I realize now that my parents showed love through their own languages: Quality Time and Acts of Service. Alas, 14-year-old Rozen didn't know anything about waiting for love, standards or boundaries. I was just looking for my person in anyone who would give me the time of day. New start, old pattern.

Sean (not his real name) was my first love. I gave my tender heart away at 14; I was so eager to be loved. It was scandalous because he was a junior, and I was a freshman. I loved the thrill of it all. I fell in love with the "bad boy" who played guitar and sang in a band called Emo Outlet. I was a love-struck teen with raging hormones. I knew he was bad for me, but I still gave him my time, attention and energy because I didn't have to be by myself or learn to love myself. He was my first boyfriend, my first kiss, my first prom date and my very first massive heartbreak.

He cheated on me with the girl with the big boobs while I was asleep down the hall. I knew there was something going on with them, but I turned a blind eye because I chose to be with him rather than without.

The Hands They Were Dealt

I took Sean back after he made a grand romantic gesture of staging my dorm room with rose petals, a giant teddy bear and an iPod which was playing *You & Me* by Lifehouse. He wrote one hell of an apology letter and promised to never hurt me again. We did the long-distance thing until he started at Jacksonville University. By then, I had moved to Sturgis, Michigan, where I got to live the small-town dream and meet my first small-town boy.

On September 4th, 2005, I moved in with my Auntie Remy and Uncle Vic. My Auntie Remy is one of my Father's older sisters. They were the "it" couple in town, at least to me. They were the couple who had a clinic across from the high school. My Uncle Vic was a hot-shot surgeon, and his wife was his head nurse. Everyone knew them. I remember going out to dinner with them and having random people come up to our table to thank my uncle for saving their lives. He'd often never remember them because he performed so many surgeries; but of course, he would never let them know that.

They had a lovely brick house in town and a gorgeous lake house with a great parking lot overlooking Klinger Lake. I can still smell the dewy morning grass on the front lawn. I had spent the summer training with the varsity cheer team, and I walked onto the squad as the main flyer. A lot of the girls hated me for that. I had many eyes on me because I was the new girl, plus I was getting tossed in the air like pizza dough. I did the long-distance thing with Sean until November 2005 when I fell for another boy.

Drake was the all-American white boy. He smelled of Abercrombie's "Fierce" and wore collared shirts from American Eagle. I honestly couldn't tell you what I saw in him other than I thought his face was so cute and he liked me. I let this boy bad-mouth me to his friends, make fun of the size of my breasts and laugh with his other preppy boy posse, yet I still gave him so much of me. He robbed me of my innocence at 16 years old. It was not consensual, but I let everyone think it was. I lost a piece of myself at 16.

Where were my boundaries? It was another tear in my adolescent heart. Sean… Drake… Who was going to stop me from letting these boys treat me this way? I sure wasn't going to. I was so lost in the idea of a perfect love that I was willing to settle for this rubbish.

Not only did he rape me, but he cheated on me twice with two different girls. One girl waited until I was out of town. The other girl was someone I actually knew and who I helped get onto the cheer squad. I helped her with her toe-touch, for crying out loud. Sounds like a typical Netflix show with teens who can't control their raging hormones, but this was my real life. As a 16-year-old living in rural Michigan with no siblings and no parents, I was free to make mistakes and have my heart broken and ego shattered.

I let Drake have his way with me and toss me aside when he no longer felt like playing with me. We dated until I was 17 and ready to go off to college. I even chose a university to stay close to him to "make it work". I applied to Hofstra University and got a cheer scholarship. I applied to USC, UCLA, MSU and University of Hawaii; but I ultimately chose Western Michigan University.

When I was leaving for the summer to visit my family in the Philippines, Drake dropped me off at the airport and said we needed to have a break. Not even a week later, he changed the background of his MySpace page to a nude photo of a blonde chick, removed me from his Top 8 and changed his status to Single. I remember calling him long distance to question his shady behavior, and all he said was, "You got the email…" I hung up, checked my email, and read a 5-sentence paragraph about breaking up with me. There was no real reason.

That summer, I was rail thin and drank tequila during the day. Numbed by alcohol, I stole from my parents' basement bar until my mom noticed the severe damage Drake had caused. I owe her a lot because she broke my numbing phase with music. She enrolled me in a musical school that trained me to be the best singer I could be. I went back to my craft. I found myself again and put away the tequila. I was refreshed, reset and ready to tackle freshman year at Western Michigan University.

I managed to stay single throughout my freshman year. At the beginning of my sophomore year, I met a boy in the woods. My best friend at the time had mentioned there was a hidden party out there. I was all in when I heard "party" and "boys." I didn't know then that the hot guy I stumbled across would be my next boyfriend, Cameron.

"Do you like to win?" he yelled at me from across the beer pong table. I respond with a very animated version of yes, and next thing I knew I was winning a beer pong game alongside a 6'4" dude I met in the woods. I wanted to climb him like a tree. We were in love but at the wrong time. We were just kids who needed a little more life experience to actually give each other the love we deserved from one another to sustain us. We weren't in a place to settle down whatsoever. He had girls chasing after him constantly, and I never wanted to have any competition. Remember, I was way too insecure for that.

In sophomore year, my sister was doing the Go Abroad program in the Philippines and volunteering in Tacloban. She met so many incredible like-minded people on that trip. One of them was Anthony. He was a 19-year-old British boy who was volunteering in the same program for the summer. When a typhoon hit Tacloban, everything was canceled, and everyone retreated to another city in the Philippines for the summer. Anthony had nowhere to go, and my sister (being my sister) asked my family if Anthony could join her and her then-boyfriend at our house in Manila.

Anthony quickly became a part of the family. All I could hear from my mom's Skype calls was *Anthony-this* and *Anthony-that!* They adored him. I didn't meet him until December 2010. Apparently, he had made a promise to my family that he'd spend a Christmas with us because they considered him family.

I remember the moment his cab pulled up to our house and I swung open the door, I blushed like a little girl. His eyes were so blue, and he had the best smile—not to mention a British accent! I didn't stand a chance. Things were getting rocky between Cameron and me, and it seemed like we were both falling out of love and interest from one another. Cameron was influenced by his friends and alcohol, and he thought it was funny to insult me and make jokes at my expense. I would cry and feel so hurt and disrespected, but I never knew the words to fire back at him. Anthony was a pleasant distraction. I never cheated on Cameron, but to say I didn't catch feelings for Anthony that Christmas would be a lie. Again, I swung from one relationship to another. I ended things with Cameron that January. By February, I was booking flights to England to be with Anthony for the summer. *Can you say "serial monogamist?"*

I spent a summer in England with Anthony. I got to revisit my old school, ACS. My old house parents met Anthony and even showed old high school photos from Chili Night (the annual talent show) and old cheerleading photos. It was a summer of drinking too much and enjoying every second we had with each other before September came back around in time to start my junior year.

Everything seemed so perfect, but he didn't like it when I'd dance like a chaos goblin on the dance floor. He seemed embarrassed of my booty-shaking and enthusiastic behavior. He didn't want me holding his hands or kissing him in public. One thing I'll never forget was him saying that he didn't believe in eating leftovers. "We don't do that." I should have known then and there that he wasn't the man for me.

After our magical summer under the trees, Anthony and I went our separate ways and maintained a long-distance relationship over Skype. We spoke every night and sent each other letters in the mail. When it came down to it, neither one of us was willing to move to London or Los Angeles to be with the other. He wanted to stay in London, and I wanted to move to Los Angeles after graduation. Before we were together, we vowed we'd put our careers first and not hold each other back. I broke up with him as I was entering my senior year at WMU. I immediately went to The Grotto, the local watering hole for us Broncos. No matter what day of the week, there was always a friendly face there to do shots with. *Numb, numb, numb.* Up until this point, Anthony was the fairy tale prince standard for me. This was the relationship to beat. I numbed myself with alcohol every day until I drunkenly met the man who would be my abuser.

I didn't know it then, but by September 2012 I was the perfect victim for Alex. He was introduced to me at a tailgating party my roommates had brought me to. Phoebe and Carissa knew Alex from high school because he was best friends with Rich, one of their friends. I assumed that because they knew him, he'd be a good apple. I was very wrong. He was more like the poisoned apple the wicked witch would give someone to die.

He was a budding professional dancer and was getting ready to move to Los Angeles (how convenient). He showed interest in me. As I mentioned, my standards were very low. I saw the opportunity to no longer be lonely, and I took it. He wasn't much to look at, but I figured if he wanted to be with me this badly, then maybe he was worth talking to. I started seeing red flags within the first three months. He controlled me, ripped apart my behavior and made me listen to how awful he thought I was. He told me I was a spoiled brat and that I should run back to Daddy. Why did I settle for this? Why did I let this be okay?

I graduated in December 2012 and moved to Los Angeles on January 3, 2013. I was verbally, emotionally and physically abused by Alex. It started off slowly, then came into full swing by the time we moved in together. He isolated me from everyone and brainwashed me with lies so much that I started to believe those falsified stories were my actual memories with him. At the time, I had no vocabulary for the abuse I was experiencing. I chose to have his love and deal with a side of abuse rather than be alone.

It was two-and-a-half years of this hell before I finally put together a plan to escape. I waited for Alex to go back to Michigan for the summer, then I broke it off with him via Facetime. I got a new apartment and a new phone. Reset… fresh start… Things had to get bad for me to finally rise up to meet myself. I had to find my power and the strength to fight for myself. After that relationship ended, I didn't know who I was. I didn't know what made me happy, what hobbies I used to have or what made me *me*. I had to rediscover who I was and process through the trauma. I went to therapy and healed my inner demons. During this whole time, I had Christian.

In the summer of 2014, a sexy, long-curly-haired Latino professional dancer slid into my Facebook messages. I saw that Christian and I had a lot of mutual dance friends in common, and I honestly found him attractive. I casually accommodated the conversation, and during the course of our messaging I couldn't help but notice we had the same sense of humor. We hit it off right away. I was instantly attracted to him the moment I met him. He made me feel so beautiful. He made me feel like I was the only girl in any room we were in. I honestly thought he would go for my best friend, the hot Italian girl with a body that would make any woman jealous; but he wanted to go for *me*.

We started off as friends who didn't want to admit our attraction to one another. Eventually, we couldn't help but to explore the chemistry further. He made me feel safe. He could love me the way I wanted to be loved. I told him I was damaged goods, but he assured me he would help me through the healing process and give me the space I needed whenever I needed it. He told me he didn't want me to go through it alone. Christian blew everyone else out of the water. He made me feel so seen and held. Eight years later, he proposed. He proposed three weeks before my dad passed away at only 67 years old.

Grief changed me. It made me look at my life from a birds-eye view. It took my dad's death to slow me down long enough to realize that I never healed correctly from relationships. I never called the shots on what I wanted in a man or life partner. I accepted whatever I got. I never knew who I was without my "person." I've never had to truly stand alone because I never gave myself that chance. I let every guy cut away at me like small paper cuts to the heart. I lost a piece of myself every time I gave my heart away to someone who was never supposed to be trusted with it. When I watched my dad take his last breath, I saw everything for what it really was. I saw myself for who I really was. I was a lost little girl looking for someone to love me because I didn't know how to love myself. Rake, Sean, Cameron, Anthony, Alex and Christian… I put them all first before me.

Fancy experiences cannot buy emotional availability. Money cannot buy confidence. Fancy experiences don't necessarily mean people have their shit together. If I had to choose between giving my kids a fancy childhood versus a humbler childhood where I'm fully present with them, I'd choose the latter. I am not bashing my parents. I'm totally aware they were both twenty-somethings trying to survive living abroad with four children while trying to make the best impression on fellow ex-patriot families. I can't even imagine doing that at this age.

This is a beautiful moment. I love the moments in life after enough time has passed when one can stop and take a birds-eye view on how they got to that moment. I know how I want to be as a mother because of the childhood I had. My siblings and I were able to have that international jet-setting lifestyle because of my parents' sacrifices and brave life choices.

My dad grew up without his parents; he didn't know how to love like a parent because his best example was a mom he lost when he was 3 years old. At age 13, he lost his dad; and an evil, abusive stepmother took everything from him. It's funny playing the cards we were dealt. It really is what you make of it. My dad was quite possibly dealt the worst hand, and he was still able to provide us with a life he could have never dreamed of. He came from a battered childhood with an evil stepmother. Because of him,

I got to live my American dream. I got to create a beautiful life with what's in my own hands.

As I close out this story, white walls, high ceilings and a gorgeous big window light my face. I have a fresh canvas. I am my father's daughter. On July 21, 2022, I watched my dad take his last breath as he lost his battle to renal cancer. The cards shuffle, and we are reissued a new set every now and then as children, teens and adults. The adult cards are much harder to play; there are more calculated decisions and bigger risks. My dad's death was also a card I was dealt. In his honor, I choose to uphold his spirit in everything I do. It scares me to sit here and stare at this blank canvas; but as I always say, I'll do it anyway.

I'm supposed to be planning my wedding reception, not planning the layout of my new apartment. That's another card I didn't want in the shuffle. Life's funny like that. I know this was a reroute that God wanted me to follow. It might hurt now, and I might not understand it, but I know it's meant for a reason. I *have* to let go and let God. I *have* to trust that sometimes I must let love go in order for it to come back to me. If it doesn't, I'll still have myself. That has always been, and always will be, more than enough.

This is extremely painful, but deep down I know I still have the confidence that got me through several first days of school. It's the same confidence that allowed me to strut my burnt, scabbed eyebrows and bad perm into my first day of junior year. That confidence can lead me to do anything, including this.

When I call on that girl and she doesn't show up, I find strength in my dad's memory of him as a child when he didn't have two *centavos* to rub together on a daily basis, yet still found ways to feed himself. He never gave up. He made the most of his circumstances every waking moment of his life. That's why I choose to honor him in every moment that I'm faced with fear and uncertainty. I choose to be like my dad. I also choose to be like my incredible mother in the way that I smile through even the most excruciating times. That's what I choose to make out of moments like these.

Life has given me so many fresh starts to transform and be a better version of myself. I am brought back to the little girl with a brand-new house to call home, a brand-new school to walk into and brand-new friends to create a brand-new life with. This time, it's just life—a new apartment, a new car and new opportunities with my career. I'm releasing my debut album in exactly one week. This feeling is very reminiscent of my childhood. It's the familiar feeling of starting anew, the rare feeling of coming back to myself and my craft.

I may not know where God is leading me, but I am becoming comfortable with not knowing. I'm becoming comfortable with leaning on my faith to get me through life's uncertainties. Change is always difficult, but I know God has something incredible in store for me on the other side of this hardship. It's only hard because it's unfamiliar and new. I haven't been the new girl in school for a while. When it feels like I have no one and nothing, I know I have my faith and myself to come home to. God has never failed me whenever he gave me a blank canvas.

The one thing I have gained from this life is impenetrable confidence and perseverance. No matter how frightening things were, there was always something exciting about being the new girl. I always managed to put one foot in front of the other and hold my head high through the long school hallways as every head turned to see who the new girl was. Those hallways were my stage and runway. "Hey, look at me! I'm the new girl. I'm cool. I promise!" Now, the world is my stage; the world is my runway. I'm still that fearless little girl.

I'm entering my divine feminine era and stepping into a new season like a phoenix rising from the ashes of my colorful past. I'm showing up better than ever as my unapologetic most authentic self. I know that no matter what I do or where I go, I will *always* be okay. I've proven that to myself over and over again from 3 to 33 years old. I'm falling in love with who I am and the better self I'm evolving into each and every day. I'm finally putting myself first and being the leading lady of my own life. These first steps in this new chapter have felt like a fresh pair of high heels I'm breaking in. The first steps are shaky, but by showtime I'll own these stilettos.

Discomfort is normal. I'd be worried if I didn't feel some discomfort during this major change in my life. I feel a deep sense of calm around this new chapter I'm stepping into. I'm stepping into my power and embracing that I am an undeniable force to be reckoned with. It's this feeling and realization that I am, and always have been, enough. I'm capable of so much more than what others have limited me to. I lean on my faith and my craft whenever life challenges me. I embrace the old and the new, and I'm never afraid to start over from scratch. I move forward every day knowing that life is absolutely what I make it.

I invite you now to examine the cards you were dealt in life and ask what you can make of them. Having maids and drivers and going to school with the son of Harrods was all lovely for me. But at the core, I don't think it really made a difference when it came to matters of the heart. I would have loved to have fancy things along with someone who could hold space for me and allow me to feel.

When people ask me, "Where are you from?" it sounds so cool. People have many questions about how my childhood was so different from theirs. I always smile to myself because at the end of the day, I'm just like everyone else. No boarding school in England could change that. It took me 33 years of life to admit that I've looked for love everywhere else except for within myself and my own company. Things were taken care of for me growing up. I never had to be alone. Life has a funny way of rerouting us until we start walking the correct path. As I sit here in my brand-new apartment, I'm entering my divine feminine era. I leap fearfully, yet faithfully, into the unknown that is my next step.

The Hands They Were Dealt

Rozen Lalas, a dynamic force, began her journey by winning Miss Congeniality in the *2014 Queen of the Universe* pageant, embodying warmth for the Philippines. Committed to advocacy, she raised her voice for *Break the Silence Against Domestic Violence*, touring the US with original music and impactful speeches at institutions like Georgetown, Ottawa, and Widener University.

Thriving on LA's stages like The Peppermint Club, Whisky A-Go Go, and the OC Fair, Rozen sang the *National Anthem* for NBA teams—the LA Clippers and Chicago Bulls. Debuting *Congratulations & Condolences* on August 25th, 2023, her Pop and R&B fusion reflects vulnerability, relationships and empowerment.

Also a senior content producer at a social media video advertising agency, Rozen seamlessly balances her professional and artistic pursuits, epitomizing the modern creative entrepreneur. She resides in Los Angeles and shapes narratives through her music and content, inspiring with unwavering passion.

Contact Rozen through her manager via email at charlie@cmi-management.com or via her website at www.officialrozen.com.

CHAPTER SEVEN

For the Love

TerryJosiah Sharpe

Ever since I was young, I have always wanted a beautiful family and a healthy relationship. I had to rely on what I saw on TV or what I wanted to believe in because being healthy was not necessarily in my family or in the families we were often around. I had no true reference I could directly lean on, so for most of my life I felt lost in the world of relationships. My actions as a friend or boyfriend in previous relationships reflected that.

I grew up with domestic violence and abuse. Needless to say, it did not help with my foundational understanding of how to have a healthy relationship. I knew what I didn't want in my family dynamic, but I didn't know how to properly navigate around it. Generational problems have plagued my family lineage, so it's important for me to find the root cause and create change. We can all recognize that there are horrible people who do horrible things and consistently get away with it because of prestige or money. I have come to realize the importance of sharing our voices and stories because they are similar to money in that they both hold power.

We know what money can do for people; but with regard to stories, it's not just about what the main character has to endure or overcome. There is an emotional ecosystem in stories for the reader, watcher or listener who gets inspired by the main character's journey. I see us all as the main character while also being the readers, watchers and listeners for other main characters. I hope my story helps you find some inspiration in this chaotic world.

My family moved around from shelter to shelter and rundown apartments in southern California. My mother and abusive stepfather, along with my siblings and me, settled in Mira Mesa, a suburb of San Diego, just before my 6th grade year. It was nice and felt somewhat stable, but the abuse I endured continued. To distract me, I had an affinity for music. I felt like I really understood it. Mom would always tell me I wasn't that good and that there wasn't a career in it, so my hopes of a music career died in high school. She was our church's music director, and she would put together shows, plays and concerts; she was that good. She was classically trained and knew the art of Jazz. To hear from her that I wasn't good enough must have surely been true (or so I thought), but I knew I had a creative mind.

At the time, fashion was really starting to take off in the Black community, especially during the end of the Jordan era in basketball. I thought fashion might be an industry I could explore, since I was told music was not an acceptable pursuit. I graduated high school in June 2001 and was ready to apply to FIDM to pursue that industry after taking a year off from high school. Then 9/11 happened, and I was fully activated. If someone had the audacity to try to take away our freedoms, I would have the absolute desire and honor to fight back for this country. I had just turned 18 on September 8th, so I joined the US Army and found myself in basic training on September 17th, just six days after those horrific attacks.

I volunteered for five years, but back then the Army had this thing called Stop Loss, where they had the option to not honor an enlistment contract in order to retain a soldier for their own desire. Their desire was another tour to Iraq for me. After my first tour of war in the battle of Fallujah, I felt I had fulfilled my duty and served in the exact capacity of why I joined. I fought for freedom, but war is chaos to be quite frank, and I did not want to go back. I understood my commitment, though, and will always honor my country.

Having been involuntarily Stop-Loss'd, I served another tour of war and was deployed to Iraq again. Deployment number 2 was just as chaotic as the first, and I'm grateful I made it out of both with my life and my limbs. After this last tour, I finally received my honorable discharge and ended my military career after six years of service. I gained a strong sense of discipline, intentionality, work ethic and duty. That military ethos helped mold me into the person I am today.

During my military service, I was able to find my way into the circles of creative people who were also musically and artistically inclined. I even helped put together and vocally arrange the *National Anthem* for my graduating class from basic training and AIT. Once I transitioned out of the military, I was ready to tap back into that mindset. When I first enlisted, I didn't ask for a signing bonus; I asked for the maximum amount of money for school. I wanted to take advantage of a free education; and about a year after my discharge, I enrolled in the University of Texas at El Paso. My desire for music never stopped, so when I found out after my assessment test that I could major in music, I jumped at the chance. I also knew I wanted to get stronger at writing, so I majored in both music history and creative writing. It reignited my desire to jump into a music career. Off I went!

In my sophomore year of college, my professor asked me to enroll in a competition. He didn't explain its full context, but I reluctantly obliged and crafted a song with classmates and other students. That song won me the title of Texas College Songwriter of the Year, an accolade I never saw coming or had even tried to pursue. It was a beautiful surprise and allowed me to really understand that I had a place in the industry. I felt like Rookie of the Year. This award helped shine light on me as a songwriter, and I gained recognition from both major and independent record labels. I felt

I had finally arrived! After careful consideration, I chose to sign with an Indie label that shared the core values I saw in myself. It was pretty epic.

Over the two years I was signed, I learned more about the music industry, worked with legends in the game, created alongside up-and-coming artists, went on multiple tours and really dove into the business side of the industry. I never got paid, but I also never had to pay for studio time, the knowledge I received or the experiences I got to enjoy. These were all life-changing and informative, and my sponge mind soaked it all up.

The interval from my military separation to college graduation was six years. During that time, I thought I was trying to find myself. My life was hectic, wild and crazy. I was a complete tornado and disaster to those around me. Here was this combat veteran doing really well at growing his net worth in college and strongly kick-starting his music career, but he'd completely lost his sense of self-direction. All my relationships suffered because of it.

I've always wanted a beautiful family and a healthy relationship, but I never knew how to get there. I knew how to get women but never how to hold onto them. I honestly didn't know how to *have* a relationship or what my role was supposed to be. I was a product of my environment. In our society, I thought that whenever I found a woman, I could tell her to jump and she would ask, "How high?" It seemed like having property, and that's how I moved in my relationships. I needed an accessory instead of a companion. I thought that if I never put my hands on a woman, she was in a good situation with me. I could lie, cheat and demean as long as I never hit her. It was a horrible mindset. I felt I could do anything in a relationship as long as I didn't physically abuse them, and I lost out on those relationships early on.

I unintentionally became an abuser. I didn't fully understand that abuse was using anything to gain power and control in a relationship. The whole time, I was trying to figure out why my relationships weren't working out. I didn't want anything serious because I was never willing to listen or compromise or work on the relationship. I felt I couldn't trust my partners because I was unable to trust myself. Three important pillars of a healthy relationship are trust, communication and boundaries. I was unwilling to support those because I was under the mindset that as a man, I was supposed to receive and not give.

As relationship after relationship failed, I was finally forced to look in the mirror and face myself to see what I was doing. In my senior year of college, I recognized traits I didn't like about myself and made the decision to abstain from all relationships so I could explore my thoughts on manhood. It helped me gain all kinds of clarity in various areas of my life. One of those was my misunderstanding of what it meant to be a man in today's society. My vision was skewed, so taking this time for myself was an important step to clearing that up. Once I graduated, I moved back to my hometown of San Diego to start my business and continue my career as a singer/songwriter.

Within a couple of weeks after moving back home, my brother asked me to attend a meeting to discuss how he could help the executive director of a domestic violence organization raise awareness for their cause. I was always anti-abuser; until that point, I had never identified as one, so I was excited to learn more. Maybe I could help shed light on DV through music. The meeting was incredible. The executive director was poised, beautiful, confident and ambitious. She was a survivor herself, which is why she started the organization. She wanted to provide unconventional resources that she would have wanted or needed while being a victim.

I didn't know how much my life would change after that meeting. I had just moved back home after graduating college, where I held the chapter president role of my Kappa Alpha Psi fraternity. Now I was throwing out all my ideas on what we could do to raise awareness for her passion because I wanted to show this beautiful woman that I had value. We bounced ideas

The Hands They Were Dealt

around so long that I forgot my brother and his manager were even in the meeting. We presented a song to her and the organization through *Songs for a Cause,* using music to raise awareness. It blew my mind to see someone with such passion go through such horrific hardships and still find ways of using that journey to help other people avoid going through similar experiences. Her name is Kristen Faith, and she changed my life by simply existing.

The very next day, Kristen came to the studio to watch us create the song and dropped off T-shirts we would eventually wear in the music video. Over the next couple of months, we were inseparable. She gave me a bunch of literature on domestic violence on how to identify red flags and warning signs and what abuse really is. It wasn't until I started diving into the literature that I learned I'd been a perpetrator of abuse in many ways, though not physical; I thought abuse was *only* physical. I never thought people could actually hurt others by demeaning them or making them feel unworthy and invaluable.

I learned that the power in our words is very important. Hearing from people we love about how much we suck or can't do something or that we're "not good enough to be in the music industry" forces us to believe those words. There are many more abusive elements than just the physical. I hope I can help more young men learn and understand that.

Kristen's desire to help me learn allowed us to kick-start a conversation about who I used to be and how that story could help people around the world. Then came our speaking journey which began in 2015, going from city to city spreading a message from both a victim and abuser perspective. It has literally impacted lives for the better. By sharing these stories, Kristen and I have been able to identify more ways of growing and building a healthy relationship with each other.

As of this writing, we have been together for 12 years. We married four years ago, and we still find new ways to develop and grow our relationship. As I mentioned before, I have always wanted a beautiful and healthy relationship but didn't always move in that direction. Now I realize how to do it. I am grateful for having found a woman who helped me understand how to do it and who also pushes me to keep an open mind as our relationship continues to blossom.

Life is as beautiful, or chaotic, as we make it. If we're unaware of the chaos we invite in, it can easily disguise itself as something normal. As active citizens in this beautiful and exhausting thing we call life, please do your best at always trying to keep an open mind. Understand that we don't have all the answers to everything, but we can always try to do our best.

The Hands They Were Dealt

TerryJosiah Sharpe, a Combat Veteran and the visionary CEO of Anthem Music Enterprises, has been a driving force in shaping the arts and entertainment landscape in Olympic City, USA for over half a decade. In his role, he leverages the power of music and art to foster a positive impact within the community. Hosting inclusive events like the Olympic City Lock-ins, he also advocates for equal pay for artists and creators, actively unifying diverse communities through the transformative art of music and entertainment.

Beyond his CEO responsibilities, TerryJosiah is deeply involved in community initiatives. As a coordinating member of the Southern Colorado Juneteenth Festival, a board member of CONO and a participant in the COSILoveYou City-Wide Worship planning committee, he tirelessly works toward community enrichment.

TerryJosiah volunteers as a worship leader at Discovery Church Colorado and proudly serves as an ambassador for the Mt. Carmel Veteran Service Center. Throughout the front range, he has elevated the music industry, adopting it as a powerful tool for healing and expression.

CHAPTER EIGHT

From Pain to Purpose: My Story of Resilience

Kristen Sharpe

To the little girl who lives inside me:

I wish I could have nurtured your gentle heart.
I wish I could have held space for you when you felt afraid.
I wish I could have held you in my arms and
wiped away your precious tears
and reminded you, my sweet girl,
that one day everything would be okay.
You'd be proud of the woman I've become.
I learned to stand tall, and I redefined what it means to be strong.
Everything happened for a reason.
It didn't make sense then, but it does now.
You're safe now, my sweet girl.
Here's to inspiring the world.

Welcome to my life. I'm going to take you on a journey of self-discovery. This story is filled with trauma, pain, healing and ultimately growth. The best place to start is where it all began. I'm going to take you inside my safe place and open up the doors to give you an inside look at how I became the fearless woman I am today.

Everyone deserves a safe space, somewhere they can go to escape the noise. Parents love to joke about hiding in the bathroom to unplug and get away from their children. It's the quiet time that allows us to decompress and reflect in peace. When I was a child, my safe place was my closet. I had a big walk-in closet full of clothing racks and cubby-like shelves stacked all the way to the ceiling. I filled each cubby with toys, books, clothes and shoes. I remember writing my first crushes' names in tiny type inside my closet so my parents couldn't see. My closet was big enough for me to lie in and was a perfect place for me to hide when I was afraid or needed to escape.

Trauma affects everyone differently. Some feel therapy is the best medicine to heal and process childhood wounds, while others run like the wind from traditional counseling because of personal misconceptions or cultural ideals. I remember going to therapy as a child and not feeling comfortable enough to open up to the stranger on the other side of the table. I remember after each session how the therapist would tell my mom, "She's fine. All she talked about was how fat her dog was."

How can a painstakingly shy 10-year-old girl open up to a stranger who knows nothing about her or her family? How could those therapists hold space for me as a little girl? Did they nurture my heart? Did they ask the right questions? Why didn't they get to the roots? These questions racked my brain over the years just enough for me to eventually learn how to hold space for myself, uncover and process my own wounds.

I know those folks didn't understand me; honestly, many therapists I've seen throughout my life did not. I had one therapist tell me to run away because my parents were terrible. What kind of advice is that? Subconsciously, I wonder if that therapy session was a seed planted in my garden of promiscuity and rebellion during my late teen and early adult years.

I vividly remember being the long-haired, brown-eyed girl who was quiet and timid. She loved homemade chocolate chip cookies, playing dress-up and role playing with Barbies. She was sweet and sassy and could hold her own without question. She was tiny but mighty. She kept to herself and had a secret she didn't tell anyone.

From Pain to Purpose: My Story of Resilience

Five million children witness domestic violence every year. Unfortunately, many of those children are also victims of mental, emotional or even physical abuse. Domestic violence occurs every 90 seconds in homes all across America, and many of those stories go untold.

Little Me

Screams, cries, crashing sounds and loud TVs masked the anger that lived within the walls of my childhood home. My dad struggled with his own demons, and my mom braved the pain and abuse to keep our family together. My mom would leave, come back, leave again, then stay. I didn't understand this cycle, and I honestly didn't want to. I was angry. I hated the back and forth, the gifts, the flowers, the uncertainty. I hated that I was in the middle of it all. I hated trying to stand up for myself but feeling like my voice didn't matter anyway. It was my parents' battle to face, and I was just watching on the sidelines.

I remember when the police showed up to our house. My brother and I were told not to say anything—you know… *what happens at home stays at home.* Over time, I became numb to it. I was convinced all families and relationships were like this. My first impression of marriage was what I saw growing up. My dad had a hard time communicating and expressing his feelings in a way that was conducive to growth. My mom balanced the weight of the world, the family and taking care of children with maintaining a full-fledged career with AT&T—all while enduring abuse. She was the epitome of strength. I've always looked up to my mom for being strong, resilient and committed. This admiration subconsciously taught me what relationships were supposed to look like. Little did I realize this was actually domestic violence.

As I grew up, I began to find my voice and my confidence. I enrolled myself into the Miss San Diego Outstanding Teen Pageant and won. I continued to compete, both winning and losing, but nonetheless stepped outside my comfort zone and found my voice every step of the way.

Trigger Warning

I went from despising abusers to losing myself in multiple toxic relationships all through my teenage and younger adult years.

The underlying theme was insecurity, both for me and the people I chose to be in a relationship with. I chose broken young men who asserted their control over me mentally, verbally, financially and sexually.

From age 16 to 22, I didn't know my worth. I called that girl "KP." I was wild, reckless and made poor decisions. I was searching for love in all the wrong places. I didn't have the tools or emotional stability to see that the void I felt was internal. I was begging for love when I should have been chasing my own heart. I learned the hard way that strangulation, suffocation, death threats and stalking weren't really love. I thought if I loved them hard enough they would change, but abusers can only change when they take accountability for their own actions.

I was convinced from a young age that the behaviors I saw growing up were normal. I thought all parents viciously fought, made up, fought, then made up again. I thought men were supposed to be controlling and women were supposed to do whatever their partners wanted, even if it wasn't healthy.

Though I competed in pageants and had a confident smile for the judges, my self-worth was nonexistent. I was desperate for validation. I was hungry—starving—for a man to love me. I was willing to accept whatever crumbs of affection existed, even if that meant accepting abuse. Toxic relationships are almost always masked in love-bombing and a lifetime supply of false promises.

Abuse isn't normal. I blame my childhood trauma for the reason I fell into abusive relationships. It was what I knew. I thought the examples I saw growing up were normal. All families *must* be like this, right? To compound this misunderstanding, I grew up in a mixed-race family, which meant culturally we didn't talk about things that happened outside of the home.

Some people run from the past, and others try to forget it. I've learned over the last decade how to learn from those old wounds and how to have uncomfortable conversations. One of the last moments I had with my grandmother before she passed away was when she held me in her brittle arms and whispered to me, "Don't look back in the past. It's gone now."

All this time, I've been trying to make sense of those words, but I wonder if that advice was for herself. I wonder if she was telling herself to finally let go of the trauma she went through as a child. The difference between her story and mine is that I had the opportunity to sit down with my parents and learn from their mistakes and decisions. I even sat down with my dad on multiple occasions to learn about his own trauma. I wanted to understand and unravel the things in my head that didn't make any sense. I wanted to understand his perspective so I could use those experiences and stories to help other families, and that's exactly what I did.

Of course, all these things are uncomfortable, and they aren't easy to navigate, but I'm going to push through the discomfort to break these curses. Abuse has been passed on in my family from generation to generation, and let me say right now that it ends with me.

I don't feel like I bear the burden of my childhood trauma anymore. I'm nurturing the little girl in me so my husband and our children receive the best versions of me. It took me years of processing, which ultimately led me to my passion and my purpose. Doing the work allows you to show up as your best self and gives you space to be accountable for your actions and behaviors.

Breaking the Cycle

Breaking the cycle is one of the most underrated things humans can do for themselves and their families. I remember being in a leadership development program where one of the group discussions was about what we wanted our "dash" to be. In other words, how do we want to be remembered? I want people to remember me for the woman who set the world on fire and made a genuine difference in the lives of others. I want people to remember me for being vulnerable to share my story so I could teach people how to heal their families from the inside out.

When I left that abusive relationship back in 2011, I did everything in my power to empower myself to never become a victim again. Eleven days after filing for a restraining order against my ex, I started a Facebook page called *Break the Silence Against Domestic Violence*. I started sharing my story along with hundreds of other survivors' stories from around the world. I created a community of advocates, supporters and families who, like me, passionately wanted to see an end to this issue.

This courage led me to turn the Facebook page into a nonprofit organization. People from all walks of life wrote to me asking for help. Even though I had no prior training, I did what I knew best: I found answers. Hundreds of supporters turned into thousands. Before I knew it, millions of followers worldwide were actively participating in the online community I created. I never thought the pain I went through could have been that impactful.

As a victim of abuse, the first step I needed to take to break the cycle was to educate myself on the warning signs and red flags of unhealthy relationships. I had to unlearn a lot of behaviors and rewrite my definition of a healthy relationship. I told myself I would never get into another toxic relationship. This meant I needed to *do the work!* The work ultimately needed to start with me.

I lacked boundaries and I was insecure. I didn't believe in myself and didn't have a solid foundation for a healthy relationship. I had to reprogram and flip on that "empowered" switch. This meant establishing standards and making sure that whoever walked into my life knew what was important to me: advocacy.

I was convinced I was going to adopt a baby, travel the world and champion domestic violence forever—alone. I realize now this was about fear and limiting beliefs. I was deathly afraid of getting into another terrible relationship, and at one point I genuinely thought all guys were dirtbags. During the first year after leaving that situation, I was always on edge that something would go wrong.

The few guys I dated after my abusive relationship just weren't right. They weren't abusive like my ex; they just weren't good people. My standards had gone from zero to a hundred. My standard above all standards was that this next guy needed to believe in what I was trying to accomplish with my advocacy efforts. I needed my future husband to be someone who shared a similar passion about changing the world. I didn't think that person existed. Also, my blinders were up, and my heart was guarded. God knew the only way a new partner could be introduced into my life was in my dreams, and that's literally what happened. I remember seeing a silhouette of a guy in my dreams. I could see his height and complexion, and somehow I could feel his energy. In my dream my guard was down, my heart was open, and I felt safe. I couldn't see his face, but weeks later when he walked into that bakery in San Diego, I recognized that feeling. "I knew I had to have him." Those were the exact words I said to him on our wedding day as we reminisced about our first encounter.

My motto is "From Trauma to Triumph." After everything I've been through, I could have allowed my past to define me. Instead, I've spent the last decade redefining what happened to me. I embarked on a life-long journey to understand myself, my parents and my family as a whole. There's a lot to unwrap, but it's okay. We have a lifetime to go. As you navigate through your story, be kind to yourself. It's hard to bounce back from trauma, but it's even harder to sit in it. Childhood wounds don't just disappear. You must do the work, or you'll notice unhealthy choices and behaviors sprouting like weeds in your garden.

Learn to turn your pain into purpose. It's the route that takes you toward healing and deeper meaning in life.

My safe place

When my husband and I started dating, people referred to our relationship as a train wreck ready to happen. Others said it wasn't a good idea for two people with Post-Traumatic Stress Disorder (PTSD) to be together. Never judge another relationship by its proverbial cover; let the people in the relationship do that.

I met TerryJosiah during a business meeting to talk about a song he and my friend, JJ Sharpe, had written. They wanted to dedicate it to the nonprofit I started. We met inside of a quaint Asian bakery located in San Diego.

TerryJosiah, JJ and JJ's manager sat across the table from me to talk about the unveiling of *Better Days*. The guys proposed the idea of creating a song while wearing Break the Silence merchandise in their music video. I was overwhelmed at the support for the cause. I agreed with flying colors.

The following day, I delivered the shirts to the recording studio. I hung out for a while and later found out from Jaz, the recording engineer, that TerryJosiah and I were a match made in heaven based on our Zodiac signs. I laughed but listened to Jaz describe the freakishly true characteristics of a Cancer and why that's a perfect pair for a Virgo.

In pure Kristen fashion, I pulled out my phone and handed it over to TerryJosiah to read my story. It was the Declaration from my restraining order that I had shared on Facebook. He read intently, then looked at me and asked, "This is your story?" I knew whoever I dated needed to know me and the bags full of trauma I held. This was a core requirement of mine that I needed in a partner. I didn't know how he was going to react. I was usually met with backlash or people feeling sorry for me when I opened up about my story. I share my story because I want people to understand domestic violence. I think sharing stories is the best way to do it.

The next moments were game changers. He texted himself from my phone, *This is your future wifey,* then walked me to my car like the gentleman he still is. It felt like a movie when he hugged me. Our cheeks touched, and butterflies filled my stomach.

We found ourselves on our first date the following day, and we've been inseparable ever since. We spent most of our time together and still do. We're best friends, but the journey to forever wasn't easy.

Early in our relationship, I found myself in a full-blown panic attack. I was in a fetal position on his bed with ugly tears running down my face. Instead of telling me to stop crying or asking me questions in that moment, he rubbed my back. He held me and made me feel safe.

Over the next few years, we spent countless nights talking about our past relationships, childhood, family and everything in between. We were able to be vulnerable together and create a safe space to be heard and understood. That's all I ever wanted in a relationship. This stranger-turned-soulmate learned how to gain my trust, nurture my heart and communicate even when it was uncomfortable.

We are still writing our definition of relationships and marriage. Every day brings a new opportunity to be challenged and to learn something new about ourselves and one another. That's what I love about us. We don't have a cookie-cutter relationship. As in every relationship, we've had our fair share of challenges, borderline breakups, heated arguments and disagreements; but at the end of the day, we intentionally choose to always fight for each other. He is my person.

Everyone deserves to feel safe, from children to spouses to our pets. The days of walking on eggshells are far behind me now. At random moments, I have found myself unpacking trauma as if I had stuffed it into a closet and it randomly seeped out. When it does, I'm equipped to hold it, look at it and put it back down. I'm not attached to the pain anymore.

I'm safe now.

For over a decade, Kristen Faith Sharpe has inspired millions with her strength, leading innovative digital initiatives empowering women and combating domestic violence. Her triumph over adversity fuels advocacy, and she has been featured on major platforms like *NowThis, Huffington Post, Yahoo, Bustle, New York Post, Glamour Magazine* and *ESPN*, sparking global conversations on abuse and generational trauma.

Kristen's impact extends to numerous awards, including *Glamour Magazine's* Everyday Hero Award, the American Red Cross Humanitarian Award, and being highlighted in the Colorado Springs *Business Journal's Women of Influence.*

Kristen serves on the Board of Trustees for Leadership Pikes Peak and Centro De Familia and is also an ambassador for Mt. Carmel Veteran Service Center. She is also the creative force behind ventures like Boss Babe Networking, The Nonprofit Makeover and Anthem Live Studios. She continues to make a difference with resilience and dedication.

Follow Kristen Faith on social media at @iamkristenfaith.

CHAPTER NINE

A Brush with Death:
Embracing a Second Chance

Noelle Peterson

I am a wife, mother, friend, author, coach and speaker. Over the years, I have been a missionary's wife, pastor's wife and a company employee. I do my part in any situation that comes up because I feel I'm meant to. I have been blessed with good health; I've had little need for doctors beyond regular check-ups.

One day in 2021, I found myself lying on a gurney in a local emergency room waiting to find out why I didn't feel right. We had been waiting about an hour with no answers. Multiple test results produced more questions than answers for the physicians, and there was no applicable family history to reference.

After 48 years of a relatively healthy lifestyle, my husband and daughter now saw me intubated in ICU after having emergency open heart surgery. I had been in the hospital before, but nothing major. I've had broken bones and female procedures as well as elective surgery. For me, this was just another surgery that would fix something wrong. I did not grasp the gravity of my situation.

I had started work one day after our morning walk and breakfast. After two hours I suddenly got a sharp pain in my neck and another in my chest. It was unlike any pain I had ever experienced. Just as my husband, Robert, was leaving the house, he realized the pain was significant and told me to inform my boss I would be leaving to get it checked out. However, I was too confused to type accurately in the chat window. I somehow texted her and my coworker from my phone that I was heading to the ER. Robert loaded our stuff into the car and attempted to walk me out to the car, but my legs weren't responding.

As he called 911, he had me sit down on the floor, but I was uncomfortable and couldn't sit still. He helped me lie down, which was a little better. I did not know what was going on and just wanted it to stop. I shifted from side to side hoping to relieve the pressure.

When the paramedics arrived, they checked my vitals but couldn't determine what was going on. I looked okay based on their readings. They helped me up and asked me to walk to the ambulance. I tried to tell them I couldn't walk, but they took my arms and guided me.

I managed to walk to the ambulance while my husband and neighbors watched, unsure of what was wrong. The paramedics did an EKG which looked normal. They told Robert that he could take me in his car if he wanted. He understood how uncomfortable I was and realized I needed to go soon, so he told the paramedics to take me and that he'd follow.

Once inside the ambulance, the paramedics allowed me to lie down. They gave me an IV, but there was nothing else they could do because they could not tell what was happening.

In the ER, my vitals were checked again, and I was asked more questions. I was very uncomfortable; I felt like there was a nerve issue as my left leg really felt like it was going numb. A medic came in next and took a chest X-ray. Then I was given a gastrointestinal concoction, which I assumed was to calm an upset stomach or irritated throat.

After a while, they asked if I could sit still for a CT scan. I hadn't been able to sit still for over an hour, so I wondered how they thought I could now. They decided to give me some Dilaudid to help me be still for the scan.

They wheeled me to a room down the hall, then set me inside a circular machine and talked me through the procedure. I remember feeling incoherent and really trying to lie still.

After the CT scan, they wheeled me into the hallway to await transport back to the ER. I finally felt like I had found a comfortable position. I realize now that it was the painkiller, but at least I was able to lie there and almost sleep.

When I got back to the ER, the room turned into a real-life *ER* TV drama. Doctors and nurses were speaking quickly about what needed to be done. My husband, who had been taking notes since we got here, couldn't keep track of all that was going on. It was too intense and happening too fast. He stopped trying to take notes and focused on praying for me. They rushed me into open heart surgery to reconstruct my aorta. It had separated and needed to be repaired before a life-threatening aneurysm could occur. Robert called our children to let them know I had gone into surgery.

The surgeons put me on a bypass, lowered my body temperature to 80 degrees and replaced the aorta from my heart up to what they call the arch with Dacron, about 4 inches of artificial hose. My family and friends prayed during the six-hour surgery. When my husband and daughter were finally allowed into the ICU to see me. I was intubated, on a ventilator and had many IVs, but I was alive and recovering.

I awoke the next morning groggy and grateful, not knowing what had been done. My husband got there as soon as he could. He spent the next 12 days taking care of our dog, catching up on sleep and spending time with me in the hospital. Nothing else mattered to him. As an entrepreneur, he was able to keep his business and podcast running without much attention. We learned about aortic dissection. I was not interested in eating and was not able to walk much. Life as we knew it was changing.

On day 6, I was taken down for another CT scan, this time of my head. I was having light sensitivities, and they wanted to check my head. Thankfully, there was nothing wrong there. They did see unusual images in the downward portion of my aorta, though. They ordered a full CT which they sent to a vascular surgeon for an opinion.

After waiting all day, we were visited by a specialist who could correct aortic dissection issues, even up to 10 years after scar tissue had formed. She spent over 30 minutes explaining to us what she wanted to do. I was ready to sign. I knew I needed to have something else done to help me feel normal.

The next day I went in for another procedure. This surgeon inserted a 32-cm-long stent through my femoral arteries. This opened up the remaining aorta, allowing the blood to flow where it was needed to reach the organs and limbs that require it.

That procedure corrected many of the remaining issues inside me and allowed me to begin to feel more normal. The circulation in my body had been corrected and all the odd feelings and inabilities I had were leaving. I woke up wanting to eat, ready to walk and ready to get home. This second procedure also allowed the medicines to control finally my blood pressure.

My husband immediately could see improvement in my demeanor and presence. I was alert and able to understand the situation much better. I no longer needed as much pain medicine, and although they were still monitoring my blood pressure, they did not need to constant adjust the medication.

After 13 days in the hospital's cardiac ICU and care center, I was discharged to recover at home. I needed some time for my blood pressure and heart rate to normalize as the medicines were adjusted.

I spent another five and a half months recovering from the trauma of the surgery. My chest had been split open, so I was unable to twist, turn or use my body's core muscles.

At no point during all this did I fear for my life. I did not know I was in danger. I am very grateful for the hands that worked on me and fixed me in those 13 days. Most of all, I am grateful for my husband. He knew something was wrong that first day, and he did everything he could to help me—taking me to the ER, staying by my side, doing all the house chores, and loving me through a near death experience.

After two months I was getting stir-crazy, so I went back to work. I worked from home, so it wasn't much of a transition. I was able to see my friends and coworkers and help them with what I could. However, I wanted something different. Life wasn't the same.

After a few months of trying to work, I began to think about what I wanted to do next in life. I needed to do more. I tried to do some activities we had found online, hoping that something would magically tell me what I should do with my life and where I should be headed. I didn't know, but maybe someone else did.

I struggled to find my calling. I struggled to figure out who I was supposed to be. I was sitting at the kitchen table at age 49 and wondering what I was supposed to do. *Doesn't anyone else know what I'm supposed to do in life? Can't someone just tell me?*

I subconsciously realized that perhaps I was missing something. I was Robert's wife, Niqelle and Russell's mother; but I didn't know who *Noelle* was. I had attended college online. I had worked whatever job needed to be done wherever we were in life. I felt I led a normal life. Nothing I did was extraordinary. I didn't have any missing limbs or mental health issues. I didn't have any stories worth telling. I never evaluated what I wanted, who I was or what I was skilled at or meant to do. I had spent so many years taking care of others and doing what needed to be done. I never looked at *me*.

After my surgeries, I wrote down these perspectives so I would remember them and be accurate when I told people what had happened to me. After mentally processing my surgery experience, I realized my whole life was my story. It may be ordinary to me, but it's what brought me to that point in my life, and it was worthy of telling. No one else had lived that life.

I turned an unfortunate incident into something fortunate. I began to look within to see who I really was. My story contained life events that both happened and did not happen. This was the hand I had been dealt. How I dealt with those things and how I learned from them are experiences that helped me grow and become who I was meant to be.

I have had scars on my body since I broke my leg at age 13. They have never bothered me. They are part of who I am and remind me of what happened at different times in my life. They are beauty marks that the world and our Lord have molded into me. I am honored to show my scars and share my story, especially if it can help other people learn and grow from their stories and scars.

This experience has reminded me of my desire to be a woman of influence. I was unable to put it into words prior to this realization, but it came from wanting to be on stage with other women when I attended a Women of Faith event in 1998. I have learned that we all have a story. We all have a reason to be on this earth. We are here for a purpose, and each one of us has a unique set of experiences and skills to do the task the Lord has given us.

To us, our story may seem ordinary; but no one else has our experiences, and they do not have our skills. We are all special, and we have a specific set of skills and abilities that touch our unique circle of friends. No one else can fulfill our purpose the way we can.

I pray that my story touches you and encourages you to share your story. Evaluate your skill set and experiences so you can have the impact God wants you to have in this world and on those you interact with.

My husband focused on not taking another day for granted. I recognize now that I have so much value to bring to the world. I am a great wife, a great mom, a great grandma and a great leader. All those experiences qualify me to help others. I want to see women empowered. I want women to embrace their stories and have the confidence to share them. I want women to discover their purpose and release it into the world. The world needs your story, your wisdom and your willingness to serve.

Noelle Peterson is an inspiring entrepreneur and journey navigator who has conquered incredible challenges in both her personal and professional life. With a passion for helping others, she founded Start Smart Systems to assist those facing challenges in business. She wholeheartedly believes that a positive outlook with creative problem-solving is the best way to confront any challenge.

After undergoing life-changing surgery, Noelle recovered with grace and resilience to strive even further toward her goals. With empathy and an eye for detail, she provides invaluable advice for all stages of the entrepreneurial journey, from developing a comprehensive business plan to strategizing success for a bright future. She is an inspiring mentor whose unique approach will help you confidently take your story and business to the next level!

In the symphony of life, resilience
orchestrates the triumphant melody
that transforms adversity into harmony.
Every challenge becomes a note, and
those who overcome the odds compose
a masterpiece of strength, courage and
unwavering determination.

CHAPTER TEN

Unloved. Unwanted. Rejected.

Dawn Cooper

From a very early age, I felt a profound sense of being unloved, abandoned and unwanted. This feeling seemed to permeate every aspect of my life, casting a shadow over my relationships and hindering my ability to form meaningful, lasting connections. My parents and siblings are very loving; I never felt unloved, unwanted or abandoned by family members—just everyone else. Having such a loving family and home life, I can't understand why I feel this way. I was never a shy child. Growing up, I wasn't as popular as my older brother and younger sister were. They made friends easily, and I always felt like an outsider or an outcast.

I wanted to hang out with my older brother because I looked up to him. However, he and his friends didn't like me hanging around that much. I was like a gnat that pestered them. So, I turned to my younger sister and her friends. They seemed to like and accept me because I was older, but my sister didn't care too much that I was invading her friend zone. I never developed deep friendships of my own, so as a result I never felt like I fit in anywhere.

I carried the heavy burden of feeling unloved. Acquaintances would come and go, but the underlying fear of rejection prevented me from opening up and trusting others. I'm pretty sure I built a wall around myself. I was afraid to let anyone in, fearing I would only be hurt and abandoned. My dad was in the Air Force, so we relocated every couple of years. I

The Hands They Were Dealt

never had time to form bonds with anyone, even if the opportunity had been there.

In junior and senior high school, my friends were dating. I was never asked out or had any boys interested in me. I was overweight and was convinced that was the reason. I truly felt I had a great self-image and self-esteem. I didn't talk down to myself, and I accepted myself for who I was. If others couldn't see that, it was their loss. I'm attractive and have a great personality. Overall, I'm a wonderful person. I decided I wasn't going to wait for boys to ask me out. I was going to take the initiative and ask them instead. It wasn't the norm 30 years ago, but I didn't want to miss out on the chance that a boy was too shy or nervous to ask me.

I took it upon myself to always make the first move. I was always the girl *friend* but not the *girlfriend,* and I had more guy friends than female friends. What's that saying…"Always a bridesmaid; never a bride." I remember what my youth pastor said one night during youth group: "If you're not happy being single, you won't be happy in a relationship." I have never forgotten those words. I told myself I would never stay in a relationship where I was physically, mentally or emotionally abused.

I met my first husband at a party through a mutual acquaintance. He was dating my friend, but I was the one interested in him. They dated for about three months until he was arrested for aggravated auto theft. I had known from the beginning he was an ex-convict with two felonies. He had been in and out of jail and prison since he was 14 years old. I should have seen the warning signs then. Two years had passed when I received a letter from him. I was shocked he even remembered me. After we exchanged several letters, he started calling me. Then I began to visit him in prison.

After he was released, I asked where he planned to stay. He wasn't sure if he was going to return to Arizona where his family lived (all convicts, too) or stay in Colorado. I offered him a place to stay until he decided what to do. When he moved in, he assured me we were just friends. I accepted that at the time, hoping he would eventually have feelings for me and that we could make a good life together. He vowed that he had changed and never wanted to be in that criminal lifestyle again. We grew closer, but I remember him saying to me that he couldn't promise to be faithful. Looking back, I wish I would have slapped myself in the face and told myself, *"Wake up, Dawn!"* I was so happy someone was interested in me that I ignored these and other red flags.

We ended up getting married over two months later, then I found out I was pregnant. Two months after that, I found out he was cheating on me. I told him we were done. I realized the mental and emotional abuse he was putting me through, and I held true to my belief that I would not stay in a relationship where I experienced any form of abuse. I was scared to be a single parent, but I also didn't want to raise my child in an unhappy home.

Three months pregnant at 23 years old, I packed up my belongings and moved back in with my parents. I felt like a failure. I felt unwanted and unloved. Even though I called it quits, he was the one who checked out on me. I didn't want to be a burden to my parents, but they reassured me they were there for me and would help me in any way they could. Once, I thought of taking my life, but that would have meant also taking the life of my unborn child. My parents prayed for me and offered their love and support.

As I raised my child over the next 16 years, I only dated four men. Three of them were short-term, so I spent much of those years single. I felt undesirable and unwanted. I longed for connection and for relationships that would fill the void and bring meaning to my life. Time and time again, my attempts at creating long-lasting relations with men and women seemed to fall short. Friends drifted away, relationships fizzled out, and I was left feeling more alone than ever. Through prayer and my relationship with God, I accepted that this was how my life was going to be. I was whole with myself and felt complete. I didn't need a boyfriend or husband to feel fulfilled. My job was going well, and my social life (mostly co-workers) was right where it needed to be. I felt successful at that time in my life; I was finally able to have an identity.

Then, something else happened. I reconnected with someone I'd had a crush on in high school. We enjoyed reconnecting and had long conversations. We were also thrilled that our kids got along so well. I fell hard and fast, and we were married six weeks later. I told myself that this situation was different from my first marriage because we had previously known each other for a while. This second marriage wasn't perfect. We struggled to learn how to deal with each other and how to handle challenges with raising our kids. We also had his ex-wife to deal with and had to manage three teenage kids from two failed marriages. This made the relationship difficult at times.

Before getting married, my husband had said he loved how I expressed my feelings honestly and wasn't afraid to say what was on my mind; but several months into our marriage he was giving me little signals to quiet me down. He would give me sidelong glances or tell me I didn't need to say certain things. He shut me up and shut me down a lot. I didn't see it right away, but once I noticed, I started to emerge and speak my mind again.

Seven and a half years into the marriage, we grew further apart when we should have been growing closer together. He was very focused on his business, and I didn't feel like he made enough time for me. I found myself feeling unwanted and undesirable again, and I felt lonely and depressed. I felt more alone in the marriage than I did when I was single. I was having feelings of loneliness and abandonment, and I knew I couldn't stay married to him.

I went through my second divorce at age 46. I didn't know what I was going to do or where I was going to live or how I was going to survive.

Feeling deflated and shattered, I again struggled with suicidal thoughts. I actually attempted suicide by taking a handful of sleeping pills. My body went numb, I felt paralyzed, and my breathing got shallow. I probably would have panicked if I had enough strength, but there was none of that. Then I realized I didn't leave a note. I wanted to get up and write something, but I couldn't make my body move. I thought of going to the ER to have my stomach pumped, but I had no insurance and couldn't, afford to do that. So, I just laid there and prayed. *Lord, I'm coming home.* I woke up later the next morning. *Well, I'm still here, so I must have a purpose!*

Several people have asked me what my passion is. They've asked me what I'd love to do, both now and in the future. I would sit and ponder those questions, but I never had a good answer. I always said I didn't have any passions and that there was nothing I wanted to do or accomplish. I would jokingly say that I was just biding my time and waiting for the good Lord to call me home. I never cared about flourishing or changing. I was happy working for a company that paid the bills.

My second husband wanted to have his own business and run his own company, and he eventually did that. In 2016, he had quit his truck driving job and did photography (his passion) full time. I helped run his business while also working full time and running the household. I earned my Associate degree online in three months, then earned my Bachelor's degree two years and five months later. It was all self-paced, and nothing stood in my way.

In March 2019, my husband told me to quit my job and help run his business full time. I was scared to death to quit a job I'd had for almost 12 years. I had job security, steady income and great benefits; but he told me God was telling him to do this. As a faithful wife, I quit my job and started working alongside him full time. After six months, the marriage crumbled. We had already been growing apart, but this just confirmed we were no longer meant to be together. It wasn't working with my spouse that destroyed the marriage. It was already over; I didn't want to stay in an unhappy marriage where I felt unloved and unappreciated.

When we decided to call it quits, I was bummed that I'd have to go back to work in the real world. However, during those six months of working together, he taught me how to photograph houses, and he encouraged me to keep going with real estate photography. I figured it couldn't hurt to give it a try for a while. If I couldn't pay the bills, I would look for something else. In the meantime, I worked part time at my friend's furniture store. That turned into full time, but I was still able to work my growing photography business. I found joy and passion in my new career. I discovered a love for real estate photography and capturing those images.

I have proven to myself that I could find my passion and my purpose even at an older age. Three years ago, I had coffee with a man who taught people how to flip their mindset, how to change the way you think and change the trajectory of your life and thoughts. I listened to his podcast and those messages helped me turn my life around. I started using words of affirmation to change my mindset.

We humans have negative thoughts, but what we do with those thoughts will make or break our day. When I catch myself starting to talk or think negatively, I immediately flip those thoughts into something positive. It felt like a weight was lifted. Even though I sometimes still feel like I don't belong, I know I'm great at helping people, and I know I've had a positive impact on others' lives. I enjoy sharing my knowledge with people who are starting out in business. Beyond that, I just enjoy taking care of people. I'm a great mom and a natural party planner. I try to foresee what people need before they know they need it.

Not everyone appreciates this about me, and some are offended by it. It's just who I am. I had tried too hard to buy people's love and affection, but I've learned that doesn't work. I've come to accept that I'm not everyone's cup of tea. I used to feel like everyone had to like me, and if they didn't, I would wonder how I could change or how I could fix it. Now I don't care if people don't like me. I'm learning to not take it so personally or let it drag me down. I like to say, "You do you," and I prefer to be true to myself. I'm still learning how to use that for good and in ways that will be appreciated and welcomed.

I don't always feel fulfilled because it's not always appreciated and I'm not sure of the impact it has on others. But when I don't do it, I feel like something is missing. One day, I'll find somebody who appreciates these qualities in me. Until then, I'll continue being a servant. In the meantime, I've been rediscovering my pure happiness and am learning how to let my light and my spirit shine.

I have come to see myself as a complete, whole and lovable person again. I know I don't need a partner to complete me. I would still like to have a significant relationship someday, even if it's just God and me. I believe everything happens for a reason. I know that He is redirecting and guiding me in other ways. I heard a song by Matthew West in my car a couple weeks ago called *The God Who Stays*. It goes like this:

If I were You, I would've given up on me by now.
I would've labeled me a lost cause
'Cause I feel just like a lost cause.
If I were You, I would've turned around and walked away.
I would've labeled me beyond repair
'Cause I feel like I'm beyond repair.
But somehow You don't see me like I do.
Somehow, You're still here.
You're the God who stays.
You're the God who stays.
You're the one who runs in my direction
When the whole world walks away.

You're the God who stands
With wide open arms,
And You tell me nothing I have ever done can separate my heart
From the God who stays.

When I changed my mindset to positivity and the belief that I am loved, I started to feel a sense of inner peace, contentment and a renewed sense of self-worth. This shift in perspective also helped discover and reaffirm my purpose in life. In my journey of healing and self-discovery, I gained inner strength. I learned to love myself, to embrace my worth and to find comfort in my own being. I realize that my purpose is sharing my experiences and wisdom with others who are still trapped in the darkness of their own struggles.

Discovering *your* purpose in life is a deeply personal and individual journey. It involves understanding your passions, values and strengths, and aligning them with meaningful goals and actions. When you believe you are loved and valued, it can provide a solid foundation for exploring and pursuing your purpose. It can give you the confidence and motivation to make a positive impact, find fulfillment and contribute to the well-being of yourself and others. If any of this resonates with you, seek those who have gone through it and see what you can learn and change about yourself. You don't know what you don't know.

Sometimes we stumble, but if we don't know what trips us up, we can't move or avoid that obstacle. Moving forward after experiencing distress and trauma can be an interesting journey, so look at it as an adventure. There are things you can do and actions you can take to support your healing and growth such as seeking support, self-care, education and establishing boundaries. If these simpler things don't work, I would suggest professional help. In time, we can overcome many things alone and be able work through them, but some things require a professional. Remember, healing from trauma takes time, and everyone's journey is unique. Be gentle with yourself, practice self-compassion, and allow yourself the space to heal at your own pace.

"To the world you may be one person;
but to one person you may be the world."
—*Dr. Seuss*

Remember that YOU are important! We never know who we may impact—when, where or how—but that is what keeps us going.

Dawn Cooper, a seasoned real estate photographer based in Colorado Springs, has passionately honed her craft for four thriving years. Her genuine love for the profession stems from the pride she takes in capturing homes, transforming each image into a compelling narrative for sellers.

Specializing in Airbnbs, Dawn finds joy in providing a visual preview of comforting retreats for those seeking a home away from home. Prospective clients can witness her keen eye for detail and dedication to showcasing properties in their best light. Dawn's commitment to visually narrating the stories of homes and retreats sets her apart in the competitive real estate photography landscape.

Dawn can be reached on Instagram and Facebook under Dawn Christine Photography or on her website at www.DawnChristinePhotography.com.

CHAPTER ELEVEN

Choose to Live Your Best Life

Dr. Michelle Mras

"Change is an emotional journey. It's not rainbows and butterflies in a field of daisies. Change is uncomfortable. It forces you to evaluate who you are. The beauty is in the possibilities!" —Dr. Michelle Mras

In early 2017, I felt wrong. I went to my primary care doctor for an evaluation. He suspected that the traumatic brain injury I received from a recent automobile accident may have been causing paranoia. To ease my mind, he sent me to have some blood work done and get a mammogram. The lab work came back clear. At my mammogram appointment there were no lumps; but afterward, the technician noticed I was wiping blood that had come out of my right nipple. She said that was unusual and brought in the radiology doctor to examine me. He suspected a rare type of cancer called Paget's Disease of the Breast. He suggested I wait 30 days. If there was any change, I was to see my primary doctor immediately and get a biopsy.

Within 20 days, there was a dramatic change to my areola. It took another 30 days to get into an appointment to see a nurse practitioner (not my doctor). She examined my right breast and said, "That looks like dry skin. Here's some lotion." Every 30 days for seven months, I returned to her complaining that my nipple and areola were getting worse. Each time, I was given a new lotion, liquid band-aid, Valium or nursing cups for inverted nipples. At one point, she even diagnosed "runner's rash," even though I had not run in years. I never received a referral to a specialist.

The Hands They Were Dealt

It was a total of eight months before I managed to maneuver my way to a dermatologist to look at my breast. When she examined me, her immediate response was, "Dear God. You have cancer!" I cried tears of joy! Someone finally believed me. That momentous day was October 31, 2017. After a biopsy, I was diagnosed with Paget's Disease of the Breast. I cried when the surgeon told me. She assumed I was upset, but I told her I was just very happy that she found it.

When we started to discuss options, she asked if I would consider a bilateral mastectomy to prevent the chance of the cancer returning in my other breast. To her surprise, I immediately agreed. You see, I had already thought it all through and planned out what I would do. I had my bilateral mastectomy on December 17, 2017.

No one wants to hear the words, "You have cancer." We must choose to take action in our cancer fight. Allow yourself time to run through all your feelings. Set a short period to contemplate and grieve, then get back up. There is much prime living to do. Life is too short and precious to squander the days and allow darkness into your world. When you find yourself in the dark, turn on a light.

I took ownership of what was happening. I refused to feel helpless and at the mercy of what I knew could kill me. My goal became to take control of my health in order to help my body fight more efficiently. I had to mentally choose not to make excuses for my health. My husband and children joined me as we shifted our eating habits and workouts to accommodate my new lifestyle.

When I was recovering from my surgery, I met another woman who also had Paget's Disease of the Breast. Instead of taking aggressive action, she had tried a holistic approach of diet and herbal remedies. It did not work, and she continued to get worse. She finally got a mastectomy to get rid of the cancer. We continued to talk online through her recovery. She was not healing; something was not right. I encouraged her to go back to the hospital. When she finally did, I waited with anticipation for an update. After a few days, I got a text message from her—or so I thought. It was her sister informing me that she had passed away. I went through a range of emotions, fear, sorrow and anger. Why did I live, and she did not? Why didn't she act faster? I get it now; she was afraid. Fear either propels us into action or shuts us down.

Before cancer, I lived my life without intention like a leaf on the wind. I allowed circumstances and people outside of me to sway my thoughts and behavior. I was simply living life. After cancer, I now fully experience life and take great joy in the everyday little things. I break out into song at the drop of a hat. I smile at strangers and stop for children just to let them know they are AWESOME! I dance in the rain, jump in mud puddles and laugh often. Life is an adventure for me now. I enjoy every moment I have been blessed to open my eyes. I don't hold grudges, nor do I get upset. Life is far easier when it is full of joy and love.

My healing journey is ongoing. First, I had to address my mental and spiritual needs. Then, I slowly incorporated the work on my physical body during the healing from my surgeries. My mental healing began well before any diagnosis. When I received my official diagnosis, I already knew I had cancer roaming through my body. I had observed and felt the excruciating pain of Paget's Disease devouring the breast tissue off my chest. I established new habits, which for me was a huge mental battle.

Spiritual healing has been life changing. My search for a higher purpose and my desire to make a positive difference in the world has driven me to become the best person I can be. I have come to the realization that cancer didn't happen *to* me; it happened *for* me. I am a far better person now that I have personally learned that the gift of life is priceless.

Physical healing is engrained into my daily routines. Since my bilateral mastectomy, I have had eight additional surgeries over a three-year period. Each surgery was challenging and came with its own complications, yet I am still here. I see the blessing as I push through the pain and recoveries. Moving, walking and lifting weights have become my outlet to clear my mind and heal my body. After each surgery, when I could barely move, I would find some way to raise my heart rate. Now, several years later, this coping mechanism has shown its benefits outwardly as I have shed more than half the weight I carried prior to this shift. Find something to be grateful for on a daily basis. Even among the pain, brain fog and surgeries, I find my gifts.

Healing journeys are not easy, so be gentle to yourself. Cancer is no walk in the park. We have so much on our minds with the diagnosis along with the treatment plan. Do not be concerned about feeling selfish. Taking care of yourself first is far from selfish. Self-love is crucial throughout this journey. It is how we fill our souls so we can battle this disease mentally and physically. Every morning we must intentionally approach our day to live it fully and take time to enjoy the little moments. Those of us on this journey realize how precious those little moments are.

Another lesson learned is to forgive yourself and others. It is futile to hold a grudge or berate ourselves for thinking we could have done better or taken more precautions to avoid our diagnosis. There is no sense in wasting precious energy on non-productive thought processes. Let it go. If you find it's difficult to let go, find a professional to help you talk through the process of how to let go of past pain.

I have been in complete remission for over five years. Some doctors would say I am cured. That doesn't mean I won't get cancer again. It just means I am now at the same risk of cancer as everyone else. I must be deliberate in my life and lifestyle to prevent more cancer. More people should be living the post-cancer lifestyle.

Breast cancer has taught me that life is too precious to play small in the game of life. I became less afraid to be myself. If someone doesn't like me, that thought no longer breaks me. The squabbles and negativity in the world stopped depressing me. I have bigger problems in my world, and being popular or developing an ulcer aren't on the list.

The courageous actions I take now are that I live unapologetically as me. I speak on hundreds of podcasts and internet television shows, and I write for magazines and blogs. I contribute to compilation books as well as write my own. I am a professional global speaker, best-selling author, narrator, actress, award-winning coach and professional singer. It is my mission in life to guide others to stop apologizing for what they aren't, embrace who they are, and be the best version of themselves everyday... Unapologetically!

Dr. Michelle Mras is an award-winning International TEDx & keynote speaker, executive speaking coach, co-host of the *Denim & Pearls* podcast, a 14x best-selling author and co-author of 27 books. She is the host of the *Mental-Shift* show on The New Channel (TNC), Philippines. She also has speaking parts in a few sci-fi movies and has a newly released EP music album.

Michelle is a survivor of multiple life challenges that include a traumatic brain injury and her current battle with breast cancer. She guides her clients to recognize the innate gifts within them, to stop apologizing for what they are not and step into who they truly are. She accomplishes this through one-on-one and group coaching, training events, keynote talks, her books, podcasts and her *MentalShift* live stream television show.

Michelle has a background in engineering, marketing management, banking, quality systems management, benefit-auctioneering, fundraising, political campaigning and a plethora of life experiences. She has lived and traveled around the world as a military child and spouse. Throughout her travels she has studied and incorporated multiple cultures into her life.

Visit Michelle's website at www.MichelleMras.com.

CHAPTER TWELVE

The Rebel's Story

Quron Witherspoon

Homelessness is a plight that knows no boundaries. It is not a choice but a journey many find themselves unexpectedly thrown into.

September 2012 began my new era in life. After serving six years in the United States Air Force, I was stepping back into the civilian world with a supercharged vision. I had a strong passion for music and the tools to start my journey toward becoming a producer. I enrolled in Full Sail University, swiftly packed all my equipment and drove to Orlando, Florida. I took an accelerated program and acquired my bachelor's degree in Recording Engineering. I was sharpening my ears for the music industry. Little did I know, it would also be my gift for film that would catapult me even higher.

I began searching for ways to create income. I relied on my film making and editing skills to foster relationships with clubs, DJs and radio stations. The first radio station that gave me an opportunity to showcase my work in the city was *104.5 The Beat Orlando*. That's where I met Chianna, Young Scholar, DJ MK and Brittnay Elyse. They would bring in artists to host their events for which I covered video content. I spent time at night forging relationships with night club promoters and filmed their party recaps.

I worked at Apple by day and filmed events at night, and I still managed to deliver same-day/next-day turnaround times. My consistency got me so much notoriety that the entire city of Orlando eventually knew my name. My video content was posted in every club and on every social media platform. It was just the reputation I needed and the perfect playground to sharpen my skills. I was doing all this while becoming a first-time father, which was the biggest blessing of my life. My daughter's birth was the inspiration and fire I needed to be the best I could be. I was no longer fighting for myself but living and providing for my daughter.

I met Donny "Dizzy Cleanface" Flores at a night club. At the time, he was managing artist Steph Lecor. She was someone I wanted to work with, so I came up with an impressive idea. I found out where she was performing and arranged a meeting through Dizzy. I showed Steph one of my best clips I had captured of her, and she immediately showed her manager. When Dizzy asked for the footage, I promised him I would deliver the video within six hours. They were both flabbergasted when I delivered on what I promised. Dizzy had seen my potential, so he didn't hesitate in making a phone call to our industry's most talented singer/songwriter, Rico Love.

Fresh off his hit single, *They Don't Know,* Rico was brought onto the Code Red Tour with R&B legend, Monica. I was invited to a dinner where I met Rico's manager, Byron Cleanface. He briefed me on what I needed to do prior to being on tour. Since Orlando had been one of his stops, I remembered meeting Rico and his crew on his tour bus a few hours before showtime. He didn't say much to me at first; based on his stance, he was very focused. His eyes were hidden behind his Dita Creator shades, so it was a challenge to read him.

I wasn't sure if he was testing my work ethics, so I set up my gear and was ready to capture his show. I remember getting off stage that night and showing him a small clip of what I captured. He nodded but didn't say too much, so I proceeded to edit the footage. I gave him a recap within 90 minutes after the set. At the time, Instagram could only post 15-second videos. I had a good filming and editing formula for show recaps based on my experience in Orlando, so I was pretty confident in my skills. It took about three shows for him to get comfortable with my consistency and to gauge my work ethics.

Rico invited me to lunch and talked about hiring me full time with the team. Excited about the news, I did not hesitate to accept his offer. I bet on myself, made a call and quit my day job at Apple. I stepped one foot on that tour bus and didn't look back. I was finally going to capture A1 content on this tour! It was my first industry nod and one of the best impressions I'd ever made. I had become a content creator for the biggest and brightest stars, consistently getting content to my clients within a few hours for them to post anywhere they wished.

I came off tour in mid-December 2015 after experiencing what I considered to be one of the most tragic highlights of my life. I was astonished to see all my belongings in the front yard on the grass. The night sprinklers had soaked all my clothing and other items. I was left with nothing. My military medals, photos, memorabilia and other items were all gone. My suits, shoes and music equipment (valued at over 50k) had all been stolen. I soon realized my roommate had taken everything valuable from me and pawned it off. All I had left were the clothes in my suitcase, my camera gear and a laptop.

Upset, frantic and distraught, I took what was left and drove 1,100 miles back to my hometown in Baltimore. I was faced with two options: stay home and give up on my dreams after all I had sacrificed or take a chance and bet on myself by driving to Miami and starting all over. I finally made one of the best choices ever and decided to drive back to Miami to start my journey, even if it meant I'd have to live in my car. Little did I know that sleeping in my car was going to be my lifestyle for the next five years.

My bills and school loans were all overdue, and I was months behind

The Hands They Were Dealt

on my car note. It felt like the whole financial world was after me and wanting me to quit on my dreams. I did my best to ignore the noise and the distractions. My only priority was providing what little I had left for my daughter. I would have to stretch the rest of my earning to keep me surviving for a while.

When I arrived in Miami, I had no idea where I would live. I drove aimlessly in that tropical city and was eventually left with the realization that I would have to live in my car. Parking underneath the 836 McGarther Causeway would be good for shelter. For dry nights, I could pull into a safe parking area by the beach in Biscayne Bay and leave my sunroof and trunk open just enough to catch a night breeze. I would spend countless nights editing videos while viewing the beach at night in a cool breeze.

From that point on, my daily routine consisted of waking up at 5 am and heading to LA Fitness to work out and shower afterwards. Then I would head to a coffee shop or any place that provided free Wi-Fi and power to charge up all my gear. Around 4 pm, I would usually get a call from Rico to film video content at the studio. This was my time to impress the A-list artists collaborating with him in those sessions. It was also my chance to make Rico's vlog content at the same time, knowing his colleagues would see that and want to hire me. I went the extra mile to provide additional content for them while providing a same-day turnaround. This was my most valuable tool here.

At times, I would catch a few lucky breaks and spend a few days doing edits in my client's mansions, benefiting from hot meals made by personal chefs, warm showers and real beds to sleep on. I mentally treated it as a reward for my hard work, since I spent most of my sleeping time crammed in my car. Truth be told, I was making very little to barely any money at all. I could afford gas and food if I was lucky, and occasionally I could get extra hard drives to back up my content. I continued this steady rhythm for the next couple of years.

As I improved my craft, my notoriety put me in high demand as the most sought-after content creator. When I did catch a few paid gigs, I would either spend that money to stay at a motel or save it up to upgrade some gear. I didn't allow debt or collection agencies to hinder me, although at times those phone calls led to threats to ruin my credit and repossess my car.

The year 2017 was possibly the most exciting and impactful moment of all time for me. Dizzy contacted me and connected me with his artist, Zoey Dollaz. At the time, he had a buzzing hit single called *Blow a Check* which landed him a spot on tour with Future, who also was at the height of his career. Fresh off his album, *Hendrixx,* Dizzy took me along on tour, giving me access to film with the likes of Future, The Migos, Tory Lanez, and ASAP Ferg—all of whom had major radio hits at the time. It was a 30+ city tour that would include seven international countries.

It was another golden opportunity to put my art on the map, and I did! I made sure Zoey's videos were the first to be posted and consistently gave him a recap at each stop every day. I got so great at doing this that I could edit while riding in a Sprinter van crammed with five other people. We didn't yet have the luxury of a tour bus, so we lived in this van for over 30 stops with very few hotel showering opportunities.

My work eventually got Future's attention along with every other artist touring with us. They allowed me to be a behind-the-scenes official touring camera man. I captured great content and great memories. I crowd-surfed with Tory Lanez as he performed *Litty* right after capturing intimate conversations with the Migos before they performed *Bad and Bujuee.* I was so comfortable and fluid in my element, and I was having the time of my life.

One day, all the artists decided to play a pick-up basketball game where each act was basically playing for bragging rights. Many of the artist crew members placed side bets on those games. To put it into perspective, it was on the scale of a year's worth of mortgage payments for the average American. That year went down as one of the most iconic moments of my life.

The night after my tour, I crashed at a friend's Airbnb and ended up meeting Green Bay Packers Haha Clinton Dix and Sam Barrington at the same house after accidentally leaving my belongings there! When they asked about what I do, I showed them my camera. I ended up filming their party and gave them a 90-minute content turnaround time. This friendship became one of my closest bonds, and I spent the next nine months creating content for them at no cost. Haha and Sam had so much love and respect for my craft. Not only did they provide shelter for me, but as a gift they bought me a brand new laptop because the one I had at the time had been stolen. I valued those two so much because they saw and invested so much in me. I will forever cherish our friendship.

I finally felt confident enough to take another leap in my career. I decided to move out of Miami in 2018 to the biggest film market in the world—Los Angeles. In that bustling city, where dreams intertwine with the harsh realities of life, there exists a hidden world that goes unnoticed. Homelessness in Los Angeles is a brutal reality, but I was not afraid and continued to bet on myself and my gifts. I spent every last dollar I had to get my car to the west coast, and I was ready to take on the world. However, I had no choice but to live in my car once again.

I applied to live in Veterans Administration shelter homes located in Skid Row, one of the most dangerous places in downtown LA. When I arrived amidst the oversaturated film industry, all I saw was a city full of shattered dreams and overnight successes. I could see the unwavering hope unfolding through those who were homeless. They failed to achieve their goals and gave up on their dreams, choosing the streets and tents for their final destinations. They only wanted solace and a place to call their own. I promised myself that would NOT be me.

Within the first two months of becoming an LA resident, I connected with a few clients who would ultimately change the outcome of my career by catapulting me into the jet stream of working with the best of the best. Corey Calliet, Hollywood's number one trainer, offered me a position to create content for him. Within a few days I was making an impression. I was invited to the *Creed 2* movie premier, which allowed me access to working with a few actors in that movie, including Michael B. Jordan. Corey made sure to give me proper credit when people asked about his content. I was plugged into Hollywood's network, and I maneuvered quickly and successfully.

I was later introduced to Dame Dash, one of Hip Hop's greatest moguls. He invited me to live in his guest home for a few months and also asked me to help him build a production studio for his network. He brought me in to mentor me, and I learned so much by working with him. He taught me about controlling the narrative and to stay ready; there weren't many breaks filming this guy. I remember a 45-day period where we went non-stop—film, edit, rinse, wash, repeat. Without that valuable experience, I wouldn't have been able to understand the basics in running a production company. There is so much I thank him for.

After my mentorship was over, I connected with Clinton Sparks, a big-time radio DJ and Hip Hop connection. He invited me to his home to create content for his family. One thing I always valued was creating content in intimate settings; I truly appreciated that trust between him, his wife and family. Clinton is the type of individual who puts others before himself, and he did that for me. He realized my situation as a homeless veteran and decided to help me every way he could. He connected me to a judge who worked closely with veterans and disability claim cases. This was a huge help, and it helped me gain more financial benefits.

Clinton also connected me with movie star Tyrese Gibson. He brought me in to create content and opened so many doors for me by bolstering my platform around Hollywood. He made sure to introduce me to every person he encountered and every actor he met. He let them know I was

The Hands They Were Dealt

his content creator and a military veteran. He even made a hoodie for me that reads, "Relax. I film for Tyrese."

At the time, Tyrese had no idea I was living in my car. I was competing with another videographer—recommended by a close friend of his—for a content job. He stuck with me solely because of the chemistry we had together and the fact that I had fast turnaround times. I decided to keep my personal living situation to myself and focused on getting him his content.

Tyrese was one of the highest paced, hands-on and demanding clients I had ever worked with. He would often tell me in his deep voice that there was never a dull moment and that no day was ever the same with him. I would spend some days in his guest house editing and be granted access to his chef, Archie, who prepared meals for me and gave me whatever I needed to be comfortable. It was a privilege I valued very much. On days I wasn't working with him, I would have to drive back to the homeless shelter through extreme and dangerous environments. What a contrast! One moment I was in a mansion, and just like that I was back in Skid Row.

With Tyrese's help and belief in me, I finally had my very first Christmas where I could provide for my daughter. It was a tearful moment when he paid a bonus to everyone on his staff. This was the most money I had ever made since starting my film career, and it held me over for the entire holiday season and into the next year.

We all know COVID was a serious game changer in 2020. It was a seriously challenging moment for all of us when LA and Hollywood's industry was shut down. For me, it made things worse because I had been days away from joining the Fast and Furious behind-the-scenes team. With no way for me to create income, I was once again forced to live full time in the VA shelter homes. That location was far worse than where I had been previously, but I refused to quit. I did some research and found out that as a qualified veteran I was allowed to live in motel housing during the pandemic.

Chasen, my VA rep at the time, was an incredible asset to my homeless journey. Every time I needed something, he made sure to put me in the best position possible. He understood my path and was able to enroll me in VA assisted living. It was a tough program to get in, but he made sure I was the first to get qualified. It took about five months, but within that timeframe I found ways to edit remotely for clients. That helped in many ways, and I was still able to sharpen my game as an editor.

One day, I received a phone call from Chasen. He directed me to the VASH program representative who aids in housing homeless veterans. This was the moment I was waiting for after years of not having a place of my own. I was finally granted the housing assistance to help me get back on my feet. At the same time, I received an email about my disability claim benefits. I was granted 100% disability with full benefits for the rest of my life!

It was back-to-back good news, and along with that email was back pay for all of my injuries prior to being discharged in 2012. That was enough funding to clear all of my debt and get me back on my feet—and then some. I remember immediately getting on my knees crying and thanking God. I hadn't given up. I persevered through all my trials and tribulations and was blessed in return. What a journey!

A wise man by the name of Nipsy Hussle once told me: "No matter what you're going through, you are closer to where you're trying to get than where you started from. So you gotta keep going. You'll eventually reach a point where you look up and realize you're closer to your goal than to stop and turn around. So stay at it."

Let your love be the kindness that makes a homeless person believe that a soul needs something more than just four walls and a ceiling.

Quron "Q the Rebel" Witherspoon's journey began in the vibrant city of Baltimore, Maryland, where his ambitious vision propelled him from a dedicated 6-year Air Force veteran to a renowned film director and music composer based in Los Angeles. Over a decade in the industry, Quron has garnered immense recognition for his exceptional video and production work.

With an impressive portfolio, Quron has collaborated with A-list celebrities including Tyrese Gibson, Pharrell Williams, Michael B. Jordan, Rico Love, and Future. His influence extends to the fitness realm with partnerships featuring Corey Calliet, interactions with TV personalities like Terrance J, and collaborations with the cast of *Stranger Things.* Quron's reach even encompasses NFL athletes such as Haha Clinton Dix and many more.

A multifaceted artist, Quron's musical prowess shines through as he meticulously composes and arranges his own music, seamlessly integrating it into his video creations. Influenced by legends Pharrell Williams and Quincy Jones, Quron is a true visionary with a comprehensive skill set across all aspects of visual execution. His work stands as a testament to his passion, talent and unwavering dedication to the craft.

CHAPTER THIRTEEN

Unhitched

Jessi Harris

It was never supposed to be like this…

Since I was a little girl, I have had my life completely planned out. I was supposed to be a good girl, make all the right choices, check off all the boxes, pick the right man, choose the right job, have children, etc. We all know how that goes.

Well, I did it. I was a good girl, and I made good choices. I grew up in a conservative home, so my family was really involved in the church. I grew to love it very much. I did everything I was "supposed" to do. I maintained the moral code, didn't cuss (even in high school) and didn't even kiss a boy until I was 18. In Bible college, I found a guy. We met in a traditional way as I had always thought I would. Everything was bliss, and my life was playing out exactly how I had expected. The patience I had learned throughout my life was manifesting as a virtue. I was extremely proud of myself.

Everything was great until the shit hit the fan.

I should have realized that eventually something bad would happen. No matter what people do for you or how good they are, I learned the hard way that it doesn't last forever. I had been blessed during my childhood because I grew up without trauma. Maybe I was naive, but that's how the world was for me. I thought I had chosen the right person to share my life with. I thought I knew what I was doing. What a huge life decision to make for a 20-year-old kid!

The Hands They Were Dealt

In high school, I made a pact with my best friend. She and I agreed that if we waited for the right time, we would be able find the perfect man as soon as we got to college. So, I waited.

On the first day of college, I walked into the cafeteria and saw him. He was perfect. Since I didn't do much flirting in high school, my bar was low but strangely high at the same time.

We dated for 10 months. He seemed so nice during this time. The fantasy I had created for myself was finally coming true. He eventually proposed to me, and I accepted.

So, I married him and hitched my life to his. I thought I really wanted those dreams, but I felt like I was being dragged along by a horse through the mud. I didn't know any better. *Grin and bear it,* as they say; I had a sweet smile on my face along the way. Nobody had a clue that I was only pretending to be happy.

I had created an image in my mind for many years of what I thought a marriage should be like, and it was slowly fading. Intimacy was non-existent. I had lied to everyone for so long about how unhappy I felt inside. To be honest, I didn't think I was allowed to feel otherwise. I never imagined that something I spent so long waiting for would be so terrible.

Three years later, the fantasy I had created in my mind began to unravel, and I realized I needed out. Needless to say, we ended our marriage.

I did not expect something like this would happen to me at 24. My family and friends never thought divorce was in my future. I was the good girl, remember? I was the one who made all the right choices. Divorce felt like a scarlet letter hovering over my family and me. I was supposed to have kids by now. I was supposed to have a real house and maybe even a dog. *How did I end up this way?*

I had hitched up to his dream while living in a city I didn't know. I really tried to make that place my own. I tried to keep all my friends, my job and my new life. Then I realized I had connected to someone else's life and dream without creating something for myself. I didn't follow the path that was made just for me. Everything started to feel foreign, as if I was an alien on another planet. I wasn't quite brave enough to go out exploring yet. I needed safety and security. I did not belong there anymore, and it was time to move home.

Thank God I had that. Seriously. At home, I began to naturally discover new pieces of myself—gifts and talents I didn't even know I had before the marriage. I learned I could take decent pictures. I learned I could teach children. I traveled globally again.

Then I began longing for the same exact pattern I had gone through before; all I wanted was to be hitched. I tried to date, but it didn't really work. I didn't enjoy it much. With each guy, I would try to determine within the first two months if he would be the right one. I never let anything marinate. I never really gave anyone a chance. It was so exhausting wanting someone that badly. It was difficult for others to be my friend back then. I was obsessed with finding someone to hitch up with.

That's when I met the next guy. It felt like a perfect alignment of two people who were done waiting for the right ones to come along. We found each other in that unexpected way. My parents met him, got to know him and eventually loved him. Finally! This was the story I had always been dreaming of. I could completely overwrite the mistake I had made before.

He was creative, interesting and different. Surely, this was the one for me! But would he accept me with my scarlet letter of divorce? He did. I didn't realize at the time how lowly I viewed myself after divorce. The idea of being accepted by someone in the middle of all my shame felt like true love. He said all the right things, and everything was perfect. We got engaged after three months.

If you've seen the Marvel TV show, *Wanda Vision,* you know the main character is the Scarlet Witch. Her superpowers are telekinesis and creating illusions. She can create a livable fantasy within a bubble. That environment becomes real and exactly the way she wants it. That was me. I was the queen of picking and choosing what I wanted to believe. I created realities that suited all that.

Three months later, it happened again. He had made so many promises of joy and adventure that were never fulfilled, and we grew apart. I had hitched my dreams to his and moved my entire life away from home to his city. *But that's marriage, right? A wife is supposed to leave her mother and father and cleave to a man.*

I'm really not punishing myself. At the time, everyone cheered me on about it. I later discovered that what I really wanted from that relationship was a redo. I wanted so badly for it to be right. I wanted this to be the completion of my story. I wanted every single bit of that fantasy I felt so completely entitled to. I was ready for kids, a home and a dog—a story!

I wanted it so much that I got the cookie-cutter suburban house and a dog who I love more than life itself, but they weren't filling any of the holes in my life. We were both empty. He stopped pursing his dreams, and I resented him for that. I wasn't connecting anymore, and he resented me for that.

Then we had the greatest idea of all time. "Let's try for children," we said. Surely that would make everything better. I never thought I'd be the person who would use kids to fill the void, but we started the process.

That's when the shit hit the fan again.

Infertility. After six years of counseling, fighting and so much pain, we just couldn't survive it. The idea of never being able to have children was just too much. It was like a brick wall constantly falling on my head. A child was all I ever wanted; it was my fantasy. The mind-numbing pain was unbearable for both of us. So, we ended things. I unhitched my life from his.

We went through the process while quarantining during COVID. I had never felt so trapped in my entire life. I was divorced, alone and alien in someone else's city I had made my own. I was emotionally exhausted and childless at 33. *Same. Exact. Pattern.*

I really tried to make that city my own after the divorce, but here I was trying to force a square peg in a round hole. I did not belong there anymore, and it was time to move home… again.

This time, it was different. I was no longer that woman who simply moved on to the next man; I just couldn't do it anymore. I dedicated my life to *learning* the lesson and breaking the pattern.

A 33-year-old single woman should have her life together. She should have direction. I was not ready to buy a house and not ready to settle down. It was just my dog and me. I honestly felt lost, and I had a giant list of things I didn't want from life anymore.

Things began to change, and Instagram made me do it. My feed was so full of women like me buying campers and vans and hitting the road. *Oh, my gosh! Could I really do that?* I knew nothing about camping, nothing about trailers and nothing about anything in that environment. *Screw it. Let's do it.*

I checked out a few campers, practiced a little with each, then found the perfect one. I took the money from the sale of that suburban house and bought my new little home on wheels. It was just me and my pup. I finally hitched up to my *own* dream.

Nash and I drove that camper out west and learned so much together. We visited national parks, drove through the mountains and spent time alone in the middle of the woods. Being in nature made me feel the best kind of small. I was beginning to shift my worldview from simply looking for a partner to looking at the beautiful country I live in.

I learned how to be alone and still make new friends. I learned how to do "man things" all by myself—how to hitch up and back a trailer, how to read a map, how to change a tire, how to poop in the woods, and how to defend myself against scary guys. I learned how to hike and love it, and I learned how to change my circadian rhythm. Out of all this, though, the best thing I learned was humility.

That was the key. It was the pattern breaker. I needed humility to break out of repeating the same old stuff. I put myself in a position to understand that my way was not the best way. I wasn't the one in charge of it all, and I didn't know everything. The camper life taught me how to be a learner. It taught me how to stop, evaluate and figure things out. I think some part of me just wanted a husband to complete me, but I don't want that anymore. If I ever do meet another someone, I want myself to be complete and to complement his life. I never want to put pressure on someone else.

I no longer want that typical cookie-cutter life; I want to go beyond that. No more fantasy, and no more of projecting a life I feel I'm supposed to live. No more risk-taking while bouncing from one mistake after the other and letting Jesus carry me through it all.

My camper life came to an end recently; I sold it after that journey of discovery. As I write this, I'm staring at the most beautiful view of the sunset from my little house on an island in Puerto Rico. The stillness and slowness of this life is exactly what my heart needed.

I'm still single and very content. Maybe someday I will get hitched again; but to be honest, being unhitched has me so content my heart could burst.

Jessi Harris, a passionate traveler at heart and an ardent advocate for living life freely, embarked on an extraordinary journey following years of dedicated non-profit work. Fueled by a desire for adventure, she embraced the nomadic lifestyle, setting off solo in her camper to traverse the diverse landscapes of the United States. This immersive experience allowed her to connect with various cultures, inspiring a profound appreciation for adventure.

In this tropical haven, Jessi has established roí Media Collective, a cutting-edge social media management company that specializes in YouTube Management. Leveraging her digital expertise, she assists individuals and businesses in optimizing their online presence.

Jessi's inclusive approach welcomes collaboration and engagement, inviting anyone with social media needs to connect with her for personalized solutions. Her commitment to living authentically and fostering meaningful connections shines through in both her personal and professional endeavors.

Currently calling Puerto Rico home, Jessi shares her vibrant life with her beloved Great Dane, Nash.

The Hands They Were Dealt

ADVERSITY IS THE CANVAS UPON WHICH RESILIENCE PAINTS ITS MASTERPIECE. IN THE FACE OF ODDS, WE BECOME THE ARTISTS OF OUR OWN TRIUMPHS, CRAFTING STORIES OF STRENGTH, COURAGE AND INDOMITABLE SPIRIT THAT ECHO THROUGH THE CORRIDORS OF ADVERSITY.

CHAPTER FOURTEEN

45 Seconds

Tara Bush

"How are you?"

That's a question I've heard almost every day since the incident. I always respond with, "Well... that's a loaded question!"

As I sit, reflecting on the events of the past 14 months, one thought overwhelms all others: I am lucky to simply be here sitting at all. Many people won't understand what I mean by that, but to be fair, there was a time when I didn't either. I often miss the ignorance that goes with not having experienced horrific tragedy and trauma.

It was on a bitter cold November night that I nearly died; and for a moment, I thought I would. Lying on uneven rough pavement and bleeding out from three bullet wounds, it occurred to me that my son might suddenly and needlessly lose both his moms. How would they explain that to him? I was so horrified by the thought. I fought so hard for my life that night, waiting for any sign of hope that help was on the way. Like so many others that night, I needed a hero. As the increasing volume of ambulance sirens approached, I felt a glimmer of hope. *Would they even make it in time?*

It was a hard fight for recovery over the following 28 days, with small victories of healing along the way. From a young age, I had learned to be resilient. On that cold November night, this attitude became more important than I ever imagined it would.

I was born February 16, 1987, in Colorado Springs, Colorado. My parents and most of my family were from Louisiana. My mom and dad had met in high school before Dad joined the Army shortly afterward, then my military childhood began. It wasn't easy.

I had learned to deal with change and the inconveniences of moving around a lot, planting the seeds of resilience in my mind at a young age. Over the course of 17 years, we lived in New York, Germany and Kentucky before Dad's retirement brought us back home to Colorado Springs in 2004. It felt good to be home.

My strength developed in other ways, too. I knew I was gay at a very young age. In the 1990s and early 2000s, society expected me to keep that to myself, so I stayed in the closet. It wasn't easy when I finally came out, but my amazing parents accepted me to the fullest.

At the age of 27, I decided to try something I had always wanted to pursue: becoming a DJ. I was self-taught and had little guidance from experienced DJs, but this allowed me to perform in front of diverse crowds such as private functions, nightclubs, bars, school dances, weddings and corporate events.

On Saturday, November 19, 2022, I was booked as the resident DJ at a Colorado Springs LGBTQ+ nightclub, the only one of its kind in town. A variety of people frequented Club Q because it was a safe space for everyone. That night was like any other Saturday. People were there to watch the weekly drag show and dance after it was finished.

I showed up early, so I sat against the wall to watch the end of the show which went later than usual. I remember looking around and noticing there were a lot of people I didn't recognize. I had been the resident DJ for many years, so I got used to seeing the same people every week. Tonight was different.

The last act had taken the stage, so I decided to start getting ready for the weekly dance party. I went up to the bar and asked Derrick for a bottle of water. He looked at me and asked if everything was okay. I laughed and said yes because I'd normally grab a shot and a chaser. "I'm just not in the mood to drink tonight," I told him.

"Me, too," Derrick said as he handed me a water. I asked him if he was okay. He said he would go up to the DJ booth to talk to me later. Derrick is a straight-to-the-point person and doesn't usually wear his emotions on his sleeve, but that night he looked off. I knew something was wrong, but I moved away from the bar knowing he would talk to me at some point.

It was my turn to take the stage and rock the dance floor as I had done for the last six years. By then, the club wasn't too busy; but as an entertainer I've always believed that the show must go on, whether it's for 5 or 5,000 people attending. During my first hour, Mikayla (mother of our son) and a few friends were there to support me. It was welcoming, especially with the smaller audience.

11:50 pm

I decided to play a 10-minute mix while I ran up to the bar to get a round of shots for everyone who was there. Derrick was busy, so I went to Daniel, who poured me five pickle shots.

11:54 pm

I walked down the ramp to the dance floor and placed the shots on the table. I knew my mix was going to end soon, so I ran back to the DJ booth to start a new one. The booth was elevated, so I had a bird's-eye view of the entire nightclub. I remember taking off my jacket because the heater was blasting. I reached for my phone to check the time, then went to my computer to find a song to mix into the track that was playing.

11:56 pm

BANG! BANG! BANG! BANG!

I thought I had blown a speaker, so I quickly tried to figure out what I needed to do to fix the problem. The sound was not something I was familiar with. I then realized it wasn't a speaker. There was an eerie silence.

BANG! BANG! BANG! BANG! BANG! BANG!

I turned my head in the direction of the noise and saw a very tall and large man standing in front of the ramp I had just walked down minutes before. He was holding a rifle, and all I could see was the flash from his gun. He was aiming into the bar where many people were standing and working. I knew what I was witnessing in that moment, but my brain could not comprehend it. Immediately, my whole body went numb. All I could think of was to run.

I ran down those uneven stairs and yelled as loud as I could to Mikayla, who was about 15 feet away from me. I threw open the back door and reached out to her as we darted outside. The light was so bright. As soon as I opened the door, the shooter immediately aimed his gun in our direction. I remember putting my hand on Mikayla's back and placing my body in front of hers.

A tremendous amount of force hit my lower back. It felt like someone hit me as hard as they could with a baseball bat. At that moment, I had no idea what had just happened. Mikayla and I collapsed in the back doorway. We both tried to get up, but I couldn't stand and fell on my back to the ground. I could not feel anything from my waist down. Mikayla tried to pick me up, she was screaming, "Get up! Get up!" I told her I couldn't, then told her to run.

I lied there screaming in pain and looking up into the sky. I felt so hopeless and alone. I was trying to hold back my screams and breaths because I was afraid that guy would walk through that back door to finish what he started. He was still shooting.

Everybody was screaming and yelling. My music was still playing, and I could hear Rhianna's *Take a Bow.* I remember looking up to the sky and the stars as a million thoughts raced through my head. It's true what they say about your life flashing before your eyes when surrounded by death.

You start to think about everyone you love, but you can't tell them how much you love them. It was like being in a movie where everything is in slow motion. The world stopped moving, and it felt like a lifetime laying there. I sensed that my legs were straight up in the air, but when I finally looked down at my body, my legs were on the ground.

Suddenly, the music stopped. People were running out of the building. I remember looking to my left and seeing a lady holding the right side of her face. Blood was all over her shirt and pants. I found out later that she was shot in the face but survived. Through the complete silence I heard my name: *TARA! No, no, no, no! TARA!* My friends, Sal, Felicia and Gil had come out to support me. Felicia knelt next to me, crying and screaming. She told me it would be okay as she held my hand. Sal knelt down with a concerned look. The looks on their faces were not what I was hoping for. Gil ran around the building to get help for me.

By this time, police were inside the club. I could hear them screaming at the shooter. An officer came over to me and told me to get up and move away from the building. I told him I couldn't feel my legs. I remember that officer telling my friend Sal they would have to drag me away to safety past a fence. "Take her right arm," he told Sal. "I'll take her left. Let's go!" They dragged me about 40 feet over snow-covered pavement. I was wearing only a short-sleeved shirt and jeans with holes. The adrenaline was wearing off, and the pain from the bullet wounds became very intense. I felt like I was going to pass out. It was so extreme that I was losing my will to live.

When we got to a safe spot, I remember Sal holding me off the ground because it was so cold. He was talking to me and asking a million questions to keep me talking. Paramedics came over and cut away my clothes to locate the bullet wounds. They discovered I was shot three times—twice in the lower back and once in the left arm. I was placed into an ambulance along with the police officer who helped drag me.

The Hands They Were Dealt

Being in that ambulance was very surreal. I was finally in a warm place, but I felt my body slipping away. I remember sitting next to the paramedic and looking down at myself in the stretcher as the police officer talked to me there. I'd heard of out-of-body experiences, and here I was, having my own. I felt panic, pain and hopelessness during that experience.

When I arrived at the hospital emergency room, I could only see the ceiling lights. Then I was quickly wheeled over to the operating room. I remember a lady with the prettiest blue eyes who came over to talk to me. I kept asking her if I was going to die. She said, "No. You are not going to die. We need to get the bullets out!" Up to that point in my life, I had never gone under for surgery.

I underwent immediate surgery. The bullets were removed during the first. One of them had struck my L4 vertebrae, which caused nerve damage to my entire right leg. During post-op recovery, the pain was excruciating. There was numbness from my upper leg to my knee, and I couldn't walk. I would need to relearn how to walk over months of physical therapy. Bullet fragments remain inside my body to this day. One of them has migrated to my heart.

A second surgery was soon required because gauze had been left inside one of the bullet holes, so becoming septic was a big concern. They also needed to close both bullet holes in my back. Blood clots formed soon after, which required an even longer stay. After my first surgery, I spent seven days in ICU. I was in so much pain that even a bed sheet touching my leg would make me scream. They had me on the highest dosage of Dilaudid, a very strong painkiller. Overall, I was hospitalized for 28 days.

Finally, the day came when I was released from the hospital. I went home, where I was greeted with family and friends. For the next three months, it was doctor visit after doctor visit. I was on so many different medications. I went from never taking meds to taking up to nine different ones for anxiety, pain, nerve pain, blood clots, and many more. I had a

PICC (Peripherally Inserted Central Catheter) line in my arm for months to fight infections in case my bullet holes decided to not heal correctly. Life was a challenge. I had to learn how to walk again, and I lived in pain daily. I was on oxygen because of my blood clots. The challenge with all this was that my life completely changed. I went from working three jobs to lying on the couch and screaming at night because of my intense pain.

To this day, I no longer take medications. I don't know when or how, but I dropped everything cold turkey and decided I wasn't going to live off them or become addicted to opioids. I've said many times that I do not want that moment to define me. I still live in pain, but it is manageable.

Post-Traumatic Stress Disorder is real. I still experience it from time to time and in different situations. Having a strong support team helps; so does talking with a therapist. I have also had a hard time dealing with Survivor's Guilt, a condition that develops in people who have survived life-threatening situations. Many times I have thought, *Why me? Why did I survive this while others didn't?* My friends, Derrick and Daniel, are gone. It is very difficult for me to understand why I should still be here.

Anxiety is a huge factor for me now. I am uncomfortable being in large crowds and hearing loud music or loud bangs. Anxiety and PTSD go hand and hand. My life has been challenging in the aftermath of that horror, but my support team has really helped me with processing my emotions and dealing with my psychological trauma. Connecting with other survivors helps, too. They know exactly how I feel and understand the struggles we all face daily.

In March 2023, I joined Club Q's team and traveled all over the nation to advocate for the LGBTQ+ community on trans rights and drag rights. I also travel to advocate for banning assault rifles. In June, I participated in a sit-in protest outside the United States Capitol. I was joined by another Club Q shooting survivor, Michael Anderson, and owner Matthew Haynes. I had struggled for so long with adversity until I started to work for Club Q on the business and advocate side of things. We have spoken at rallies, pride events, festivals, the White House and Congress.

As the new owner of The Q by Club Q, I will make sure we continue to have a safe space for the future LGBTQ+ community here in Southern Colorado, and we will continue to advocate for change and acceptance.

I never want to live my life in fear. Overcoming fear after a mass shooting isn't easy, and I still have my days. I want my son to grow up in a country where he can go to school without fearing he will be murdered. I want him to be able to walk into a store and know he will come out in one piece. I want him to watch a movie and let me know if it's worth seeing. I want him to hang out with friends at a bowling alley and brag about his high score. I want him to be able to experience night clubs that should be safe spaces.

Throughout this experience, many have called me Wonder Woman, a true inspiration to many. However, I do not see that. I'm just a regular person who happened to be in an LGBTQ+ space that was damaged by hatred. Hate is spread far and wide, but love will always win. I will not allow those 45 seconds of hatred to define my life.

Tara Bush, a military child and native of Colorado Springs, Colorado, has cultivated a diverse background shaped by her passion for sports and an array of professions. From instructing as a DJ at an alternative high school to managing a catering company on a military base, and eventually owning The [New} Q Lounge, she has worn many hats.

Her proudest accomplishment was becoming a self-taught DJ at 27, performing for diverse crowds at private functions, nightclubs, weddings, and corporate events. Tara's remarkable journey includes opening for notable acts like DJ Pauly D, Dev, Bryce Vine, Joey Badass, MAX, Red One, Kent Jones, Hoodie Allen, Morgan Wallen, Eli Young Band, In Real Life, Aaron Carter, Lil Keke, Fana Hues, Raelynn, Sean Kingston, Cameron Deleon, WIZTHEMC, Kid Ink, Waka Flocka Flame, and many more. However, her most cherished role is that of a mother, marking a journey that surpasses all others in significance and fulfillment.

Rest in Peace: Derrick Rump, Daniel Davis Aston, Ashley Paugh, Raymond Green Vance, and Kelly Loving.

I am… Mother. LGBTQ Advocate. DJ. Business Owner. Resilient. Thankful.

The Hands They Were Dealt

Resources from Your Authors

Poems
The God Who Stays by Matthew West

Songs
Angel by the Wings by Sia
A Little Bit Stronger by Sara Evans
Keep Breathing by Ingrid Michaelson

Books
It Didn't Start With You by Mark Wolynn
Getting Past Your Past by Francine Shapiro, PhD
The Body Keeps the Score by Bessel van der Kolk
Waking the Tiger by Peter A. Levine
Insight by Yung Pueblo
Lighter by Yung Pueblo
The Way Forward by Yung Pueblo

Communities and Support Groups
National Alliance on Mental Illness Help Line: (800) 950-NAMI
The Hands They Were Dealt Facebook Page
Chemo Buddies for Life: www.facebook.com/CB4L.org

Facebook and Google are great places to search
for support groups, as well. Don't be afraid to ask for help.

DISCLAIMER

No matter the trauma, circumstance or medical issue you may be going through, recovery plans will be individualized based on specific circumstances and medical history of the individual. Please seek help if you need more assistance. This book is a resource and should not be considered advice to live by. What helps one person may not help another. The resources listed above are for informational purposes only. Consult with healthcare professionals for personalized advice and guidance.

It's important for individuals with any type of PTSD to reach out to mental health professionals, counselors or support groups for assistance. The above resources can provide valuable information and support, but they are not a substitute for professional care. Encourage those who need assistance to seek help from qualified healthcare providers.